Two O'Clock on a Tuesday at Trevi Fountain

A Search for an Unconventional Life Abroad

HELENE SULA

Blue Star Press.

For Michael, you will always be my best decision. Thank you for encouraging us to take a leap and for always going for the adventure . . . even when that means running through airports and writing books while moving abroad. Again.

For Mom and Dad, who made me skip the slumber party and go to London instead. It turns out, you were right. Thanks for not saying "I told you so" and teaching me to reach for my wildest dreams. Without you and your editing, this book wouldn't be possible.

Two O'Clock on a Tuesday at Trevi Fountain

Introduction

As I settled into my rigid economy-class seat, two looming questions surfaced.

First, is this the day I would finally break my sudoku record?

And . . . is it possible to make travel your life?

My thoughts raced forward and back as we drew above the clouds, the rest of the world grounded beneath us. It felt scary but liberating. An airplane is where I do my best thinking.

I twisted in the window seat, pressing my iPhone against the glass as the wing of the plane glided through puffy rose-colored clouds.

"First time flying?" the woman in the middle seat asked me. She wore sharp black slacks and a white button-down, so I guessed she was traveling for business.

"Oh, no." I shot her a smile and held the camera against the window for a few more seconds to capture a video. "I just think the sunrise is really beautiful from up here."

"Don't worry—in time you'll get over that," she said, adjusting the crisp collar of her shirt and then nudging the corner of her briefcase under the seat in front of her. "The more you travel, the less thrilling it gets."

But that was what terrified me most—more than turbulence, more than wearing a business suit on a plane. To become so jaded that even the sight of a sunrise from 35,000 feet in the air wouldn't compel a double take. I looked out the window and promised myself that no matter how well traveled I became, I would never lose my sense of awe.

Time. I've always been obsessed with time. Covetous of how I spend it, anxious about how the present slips away, and nostalgic of the past. I've thought wistfully: Life will never look like this again. It's a fear. A fear that I'm missing out or not making the most of my time.

In the last eight years, I've spent a big chunk of my time in motion: running through airports, tripping along cobblestone streets, trying to catch up and devour as much of each moment as possible, all the time worried that I'll never get to see and do as much as I want. I've asked myself, How can I make the most of my time, live on my own terms, and leave my mark?

Very few of us create a life we hope will be forgotten. We want to leave some sort of legacy behind—be it with art or offspring. We want to create something that lasts, but how to do that isn't always clear.

At least, it wasn't for me. All I knew was that I wanted to do something different with my life, but not so different that I had to leave everything behind.

I thought that to leave a legacy, I needed an answer, a complete idea of what it should mean so I could build toward it. I wanted a clear path, with step-by-step instructions to achieve a finished product. But I'd been going about it all wrong. Traveling and witnessing the beauty of the world in all its imperfect, transitory glory opened my eyes to the fact that you just need to start. You'll figure it out along the way. And some things are worthy even unfinished.

Case in point: la Sagrada Familia, a church in Barcelona, Spain, is more reminiscent of a sand-drip castle than a cathedral. It's Spanish architect Antoni Gaudí's masterpiece—opulent, endlessly fascinating, and it dominates the Barcelona skyline. But most notably, it's unfinished. In fact, it's been under construction for over one hundred years, even long after the architect's death. Despite being incomplete, it's known as Gaudí's most impressive work, and it's the city's most-visited landmark.

La Sagrada Familia illustrates why it's important to just start, even if your goals or dreams remain unfinished after you're gone. Because at least you tried, and better yet, maybe one day it will be your life's greatest achievement.

I grew up in a family in which pursuing your dream job was perfectly normal. My dad is a Pulitzer Prize–winning journalist, and his work has changed lives and laws across the country. My mom is the author of four books, the editor of many magazines, and, as a college professor, she headed up a successful study abroad program.

Big shoes to fill, as you can imagine.

And yet, they still picked me up from school every day and took large chunks of time off to be with me and my two sisters. They'd somehow figured out how to spend time on their terms, even with the demands of careers, child-rearing, and home life.

When I first discovered my passion for travel blogging, the only travel blogger I'd heard of was a middle-aged man named Rick Steves, who had cropped blond hair, glasses, and always seemed to have a backpack slung over his shoulder. He's brilliant and incredibly successful. And he's also a nerd who sounds permanently congested. He looks like your weird uncle.

And the only people I'd heard of who'd moved abroad had sold all their belongings and flitted off to far-flung, dreamy places like Bali. Vagabonds who didn't have a mortgage or a car loan. I got the impression that they shirked off responsibility to live a life of adventure, which was enticing but not exactly my calling. I need stability—in fact, I crave it.

So I wanted a grand life, but I also wanted to stay grounded. Was that possible? I never envisioned myself trekking the Amazon or climbing Mount Everest, but I certainly didn't see myself working from a cubicle for life either. So where was the sweet spot in between? That delicate balance was missing from examples in my own life and from representations in pop culture and social media.

This was a logical fallacy on my part. Surely there was room for social media influencers who weren't waifs in ballroom gowns. And surely it was also possible to move abroad in search of adventure but still find stability. Of course, you didn't need to be a nerd with a backpack to be a successful travel resource.

The question I should have been asking was *How can I find my own way?*

I always like to have a guide when trying something new, a measuring stick for what's possible. In fact, many of us do. For decades, no one could break the four-minute mile. Professional runners had been chasing that goal since the late 1800s; everyone thought it was impossible. And then, on May 6, 1954, in Oxford, England, Roger Bannister hit the mile marker at 3 minutes and 59.4 seconds. Not long after, others did it too. What had once been thought of as an unreachable goal became the benchmark, the standard for others to achieve, and it broadened our understanding of what was possible in the process. Where was my Roger Bannister?

When I moved abroad to a country I'd never stepped foot in before, I soon realized that I didn't need a guide to figure out what my life could look like. I just needed a plan and some guts.

Maybe I can be your measuring stick. I'm not a star or a supermodel, and I'm definitely not Rick Steves. I'm just a married girl with a mortgage, two dogs, and—finally—a job I love.

Rather than counting down the days to my next adventure, as most of us have grown accustomed to do, I decided to make adventuring my job—and to make my job my life. I quit my nine-to-five office job and plunged headlong into work as a travel blogger. I moved abroad with my husband and two dogs, but I didn't do it on a whim. I took a calculated risk that altered the course of my life.

I'm hopeful that my story will inspire others to follow a life in the direction of their dreams. Because we don't always have to follow that same path. But my story—and this book—aren't a blueprint for how to get there. No one way is the right way.

If you take away anything from this book, I hope it's that your dreams aren't as out of reach as you think they are.

And whatever risk you're willing to take? It's worth it.

Fifty Hours a Week

"Fifty hours a week? That's criminal!" An attractive middle-aged Australian man leaned across the black-top bar and looked me straight in the eye.

I had just told him the number of hours a week I worked.

The blade of a windmill whooshed past the clouded windowpane across from us, stirring me from my reverie. We were in Amsterdam, the second country on our three-stop trip across Europe. I was three drinks deep at two in the afternoon after riding a bike around the city all day with my husband, Michael, and our friend Josh. Now, somehow, this Australian man—whom I'd known for all of five minutes, I might add—was making me question every life choice I'd ever made in my twenty-five years, here in this dimly lit bar inside a windmill five thousand miles from home.

"I just put up a black sheet and work from anywhere in the world on a video call," the Australian was saying. "My clients are none the wiser. I can be in Bali on a Monday and—what day is it, anyway?" He looked at the three of us, all standing around him on his barstool as he held court like a king on his throne.

"Tuesday," Michael replied.

"Right, a Tuesday in Amsterdam."

This was mind-boggling in 2012. I didn't know anyone who worked remotely. In fact, I don't think I'd ever even used the term. Digital nomad? Virtual jobs? These words were as foreign to me as Dutch.

But that was the whole point of traveling abroad, right? To reach beyond the familiar, to expand your awareness, to experience how other cultures lived and worked. The weeks and months leading up to that moment at the bar had been a jolt to my system, had put me in the right state of mind to absorb this man's message, even though I'm sure he never realized the impact he had on me.

Months before, I'd seen a YouTube video about the extravagant electronic dance music festival Tomorrowland in Belgium. I'd never traveled on my own before, without my family; I'd never planned a trip by myself . . . I didn't know what I was doing, and I was nervous. But something about the music festival pulled me in like a magnet. I had to go.

All my friends were enthused to go too—or so I thought. When it actually came time to buy tickets, everyone had an excuse: it was too expensive, they couldn't get the vacation days . . .

Maybe next time.

So it was just me, Michael, and Josh. We would spend ten days in Europe: three in Belgium for the festival, three in Amsterdam, and the last four in Paris.

I made a countdown on my phone, and I would peek at it from the dull gray walls of my cubicle as the date crept nearer. I made a checklist and a to-do list, printed off backups and made copies of credit cards, stuffing important documents inside folders in case I forgot anything or in case I wound up taken and needed someone to identify my body.

"Don't bring your wedding ring or any fancy jewelry," my relatives warned. "Pickpockets are ruthless!"

And someone even told me that they cut off fingers in Paris. I wasn't sure I believed them, but I took off my wedding ring and left it at home—just in case.

With every detail in order, or so I thought, we strode up to the DFW airport check-in desk, where the agent looked up from my passport and said, "Ma'am, this isn't going to fly."

Despite my obsessive planning, I'd managed to overlook one tiny detail. After our wedding the previous April, I'd changed my name on every document except one: my passport.

After lots of finagling, missed flights, and questionable documents proving my name, we made it to Belgium for Tomorrowland.

The cartoonlike gates leading into the music festival looked like Dr. Seuss meets Ringling Brothers, welcoming attendees to a whimsical world for adults.

Beyond the gates a huge Ferris wheel and crowds of people from all over the world were waving flags and dancing. I was a scaredy-cat terrified of getting caught with drugs, so I didn't know what a true high felt like, but I knew this had to be close.

Standing on the hill, we spotted seventeen stages dotting the terrain, with massive tents pulsating with the beat. At one stage, lasers shot above the crowds, and at another stage by the water, a platform moved as the crowd jumped. Elaborate flowers floated atop the lakes spewing colorful streams of water. Lights and lanterns hung in every tree. Arched gateways and spinning globes directed guests to bathrooms or "refresh points," complete with deodorant and even cologne.

Among the biggest draws was the main stage, where a giant bookshelf with a massive twenty-five-story book that read The Book of Tomorrow. We watched as acrobats climbed atop books and fire-breathers competed with pyrotechnics. The continuous action carried on between sets. As one DJ finished, the next came up. Martin Garrix, Tiësto, Skrillex, Kaskade, and Avicii, the most famous DJs in the world, one after another, playing to a crowd of over one hundred thousand from countries all over the world. The energy was infectious.

With each beat or thumping base, bursts of colorful explosions illuminated the sky in sync with the music, like a symphony of fire and sound. I half expected Beethoven to jump out from behind the fireworks and start conducting.

Tomorrowland was unlike anything I'd ever experienced, and despite its chaos and wonder, there was also a soothing quality to its structure and organization. I had nothing to fear, so I felt even more free to just let go and enjoy myself. I suddenly wished I could find this sort of balance in my everyday life.

"This is it, man," Josh said, beaming. "This is what life's about."

I thought of my passport with the wrong name. I thought about our friends who had a million excuses why they couldn't come. We could have missed this.

But we hadn't.

I glanced up at a rainbow sign with swirls of red-and-white candy canes flanking its edges: Yesterday is History, Today is a Gift, Tomorrow is a Mystery.

I hadn't even known this festival existed until I saw a YouTube video a few months earlier. Now, here was one of the most memorable moments of my life.

"Michael," I said, throwing my hands in the air as blue and green fireworks shimmered in the sky, "our wedding day is here." I put up my right hand as high as I could. "Where would you put Tomorrowland?" I offered him my left hand.

"Up here." He moved my hand up evenly with my right.

"Agreed," I said, breathless. "My mind is blown."

A few days later in Amsterdam, we bought a sprawling map roughly the size of Liechtenstein that Josh and Michael hoisted onto building walls throughout the city to pinpoint our next destinations. We rented rickety yellow bikes and whizzed around the streets, trying to see as much as we could in just a few days, barely leaving time to sleep in the small hostel where we'd locked our backpacks in trash cans.

Canals snaked like ribbons through winding streets flanked by roads lined with tall, skinny houses leaning intimately inward, as if in hushed conversation.

We biked through busy traffic to a park, and there we were, in a large windmill converted into a bar where we struck up that conversation with the Australian.

"Americans work too much," he stated before swigging his beer.

Maybe, just maybe, he was right. Maybe working fifty hours a week for someone else, doing something I hated, was criminal. But how could I pull off all that I truly wanted—to work at something inspiring, find stability, and manage to travel the world, too? Where could I find that balance? Where was my Tomorrowland?

The gears in my head were spinning. How could I work from anywhere and make a living? The thought stayed with me.

In Paris, every step felt like a story, every stone an architectural masterpiece. How could I see more of the world? I knew now that, for me, ten days off every year wouldn't cut it.

As I watched the Eiffel Tower glimmer against the inky black sky, I decided to change my life. I'd travel more and live on my own terms. I had no idea what that meant yet, but I'd figure it out.

I sipped three-euro wine out of a flimsy plastic cup and felt tears prick my eyes. I looked at Michael on our makeshift picnic blanket, my scarf. He was layering as much cheese as possible onto a piece of roughly torn baguette. Josh was adding more wine to his cup. Now I was full-on crying.

Michael set down his tower of bread and cheese and cupped my chin in his hands. Despite the dark, I knew he could sense my excitement.

"We have to do more of this," he said.

"We have to move," I replied.

Sleepily, I drank more wine. The past ten days had been a whirlwind of music and lights and history and culture. I wanted more.

It was as if that Australian man in the windmill bar had flicked on a light: maybe life didn't have to be so mundane, so tedious, so many hours of work with only snippets of adventure. Maybe I didn't need to be working overtime in a cubicle in Dallas. I'd always been afraid of change, even freaked out by the passage of time. But what was I afraid of? What was I holding on to in the so-called safety of my monotonous life? Could I risk it for the chance at something different?

I made a pinky promise with the Eiffel Tower: I was going to find out.

London Lights:
Back to the Beginning

The white strings of my Apple earphones dangled in time with my steps as I walked from York Street to the Marylebone Tube station. I was listening to "Unwritten" by Natasha Bedingfield and feeling totally invincible, the way I feel whenever I'm traveling. The feeling surfaced like a fresh bubble of champagne, leaving me lighter and a little more daring.

I hopped off near Portobello Road and began to stroll through the weekend market, each row bursting with color. At one jewelry stand, I plunked down £8 for a pair of pale green seashell earrings. As I walked away, it occurred to me that no one at the market knew who I was, where I came from—nothing. It was liberating. My confidence soared and I held my head a little higher, strutting as if I owned Harrods or Fortnum & Mason.

As the midday July sun beat down on me, I wiped a bead of sweat off my top lip and unlocked the door to my family's flat. At nearby

St. Mary's School, I overheard a kid scream, "I'm knackered! Let's head in for tea." So perfectly British, I thought, and Dallas seemed so much farther away than 4,700 miles.

I'd been in London before, but this time was going to be special: my boyfriend was flying in to join me. For the past four years my parents had been teaching a study abroad program at Regent's College (now Regent's University), so once again I was spending six weeks of my summer break traipsing around one of the coolest cities in the world. I've heard people say: "London is the whole world in one place."

But I hadn't realized that at first.

When I was fourteen, my life revolved around my friends and summer vacation. It seemed catastrophic to be missing Michelle Ackels's fourteenth birthday party because I'd be stuck in London. And I was further mortified that I wouldn't be present for Tessie Watson's summer soirée. And, what about dance camp, Mom? And worse, what if everyone got a boyfriend except for me? What if something really cool happened? It destroyed me that I wouldn't be privy to the hot gossip.

I'd had to settle for instant messaging.

This is how I know that kids are idiots, teenage-me included. At fourteen, I'd been ready to push away all the opportunities in front of me just to head back to Dallas, Texas, instead of spending the summer in London attending world-class plays and strolling down Oxford Street.

On that first trip, my parents had made me attend the student orientation at Regent's. The dean blathered on about the importance of behaving like proper students, and my eyes had drifted out the window to the lush green lawn and grass tennis courts, imagining what my friends were doing back home.

Nothing the dean was saying applied to me, I thought. After all, I wasn't a student, just a professor's kid trying to keep my younger twin kid sisters from pulling each other's hair.

Then, as the dean concluded his speech, he fixed his eyes on each student, teacher, and kid, before saying, "Six weeks might feel like a long time, but it's only a blink. Do it all. See everything. Burn the candle at both ends. Remember, you can sleep when you're dead."

His words struck me and stuck. That line would haunt and delight me the rest of my life. Though at the time, I didn't register it.

Now here I was four years later, a high school graduate and a much wiser eighteen-year-old. I had begun to appreciate the brilliance of traveling, and I couldn't imagine not going on this trip and savoring every experience I could. I lobbied my parents to let my boyfriend, Michael, come along, and was shocked when they obliged. My dad already felt like he had a son in Michael.

Michael flew into Heathrow a week after my family and I arrived, as he'd had to stay back and serve as best man in his brother's wedding. When I met Michael at the train station, I immediately spotted him. The vision of him standing at six-foot-two with his thick, messy brown hair and hazel eyes made my heart stop for what felt like a full three seconds.

We had met one year prior, the summer before our senior year of high school. At seventeen, I was that ornery, self-assured girl who had no intention of having a boyfriend going in to her last year of high school. But when I saw that cute, tall guy smoking a cigar at the party, I was immediately drawn to him.

I hadn't been looking for a boyfriend, no, but shortly after we met, he not only endured a marathon of my cringe-worthy childhood home movies but began to cheer me on at every one of my high school plays. He was a keeper. And so I realized that sometimes the best things in life come when you're not looking for them.

I wasted no time showing him London's hot spots—strolling Regent Street, taking pictures in front of Big Ben, touring the Tower of London with the Beefeaters, and sneaking into Westminster Abbey.

Each time I watched Tower Bridge light up at night, it mesmerized me. The lights' warm glow dance along the River Thames, the bridge's black spires' silhouettes against the deepening blue sky. Red double-decker buses, shiny black cabs, and mini-cars far smaller than anything we drove in Texas zipped in all directions. As night drifted toward darkness, London's lights burned brighter, turning the city into a stage with a new cast of characters spilling out as if waiting in the wings.

With Michael by my side, I felt alive in the glow of London's spotlight.

The next morning, we sat on a bench among yellow tulips in Regent's Garden.

"I've never felt like this before," Michael blurted out.

Is he talking about me? I wondered. Or this trip?

Michael tends to get straight to the point. That's great for speed dating and bumper stickers, and it helps me decide if I'm mad at him or not. Plus, I like knowing where I stand. But at that moment, I didn't know what he meant. So I pursed my lips and left his words hanging in the air.

"I mean about a place." He waved his hands in the air like Vanna White, showing off another letter on *Wheel of Fortune*. "I grew up going to my family's farm and we went on some bigger trips here and there, but this—this is mind-blowing."

I dramatically narrowed my eyes.

"And, of course," he added, "I've obviously never felt like this about a girl before."

Well played, Michael, I mused.

After a week in London, we joined my parents' study abroad group for a side trip to Ireland. Early on the morning of July 7, 2005, we all threw on our backpacks and boarded the Tube en route to the train station, something I'd done countless times before. My mom, who was leading the SMU-in-London program, left for the airport so she could arrive before our ferry and check the arrangements ahead of time. She told me later that, as she rode the escalators up and out of the station, she'd heard a rumble, then noticed the lights flicker. The escalator stopped, and she climbed the rest of the way up and out of the station. She didn't give it much thought.

Meanwhile, we had already boarded our train to Ireland. An hour or so into our ride, we were delayed. Our train had broken down, so we gathered our belongings and disembarked. I noticed an unusual stirring among the other passengers at the station, and I could feel the tension beginning to rifle its way through the crowd. We huddled around TVs as the news flashed: "Bombing on London Underground" read the headlines. The bombings were what had caused the lights to flicker and stop the escalator my mom had ridden on—she had missed the explosions by mere minutes. So had we. If our train had broken down before arriving to pick us up, we would have been right in the middle of the bombing.

I watched the screens in shock. Three bombs had exploded, simultaneously destroying three sections of the London Underground and a fourth had hit a bus, killing fifty-five people in all and injuring more than 700—the biggest attack on London since WWII. London called it their 9/11. We missed it by mere minutes.

Shaken, scared, and confused, I felt grateful we were going to Ireland, where we could escape the turmoil unfolding on the streets of London. My mom sent all the students and professors on the planned tour of the scenic Irish countryside, while she stayed behind to deal with the authorities and students' parents, who were all freaking out as they watched the gruesome news from thousands of miles away. I was supposed to go with the students, but I was terrified that another attack might happen. I wanted to stay with my parents.

So my dad, Michael, and I insisted on staying with my mom at her friend J.J. Magee's house in Belfast. Once we arrived, J.J. took us to Giant's Causeway on the coast, where we stepped over closely packed, hexagonal stone columns and meandered down green windswept paths.

Soon reporters revealed that radical Islamic terrorists had carried out the four coordinated suicide attacks. I felt as if I couldn't breathe. I thought maybe we should just go home.

J.J. did his best to distract Michael and me with hikes and even taught us how to make proper tea. He gently attempted to explain the irony that Belfast, the place we'd gone to escape the aftermath of a bombing, had seen more than its fair share of violence. At the time I couldn't grasp the truth in his words. But years later I realized we could not have been in better hands at the time than with J.J., who knew all too well the shock we hadn't realized we'd experienced.

Reality set in when we returned to London a few days later. The mere thought of boarding a crowded bus or train or getting on the Tube sent me into an anxious spiral. I found myself hopping off buses several stops early when I'd spot a man carrying a briefcase. A seemingly innocuous sight now felt charged with potential danger. The whole city was on edge.

But beneath the obvious fear, I began to notice a rallying force building and then echoing throughout the city: the quintessential British "Keep Calm and Carry On" attitude. Londoners were not going to take this lying down. They headed back to the Tube, back to the buses, and continued to live their lives, refusing to give in to fear. The queen said it best: "Atrocities such as these simply reinforce our sense of community, our humanity, and our trust in the rule of law. That is the clear message from us all."

But I wondered about Michael. With all this turmoil on his first international trip, would he swear off traveling abroad? Somehow, though, the tragedy only strengthened his resolve. We both felt like we were part of something. Something abysmal, disturbing, and catastrophic had happened—not just to London or England, but to us, too. We were now connected to the world in a different, more meaningful way. We didn't have to form opinions or make political decisions, but we did have to stand up and support the city by getting up and continuing to experience the world. Just like the Londoners, we got back on the bus and we got back on the Tube. The bridge lights still flickered on the Thames. The show was still on. We still loved London, and that wouldn't change.

A tectonic shift occurred for both of us that summer. We both grew up a little in ways we hadn't predicted. All the typical platitudes about such experiences sound trite, like greeting card blurbs. "Things can and will happen." Or "Tragedies occur; it's how you cope that matters most," and so on. But for Michael and me, what rang true was the reality of the inevitable unknown, life's unpredictable turns, never knowing when your last day on Earth might be.

As much as I feared change, as much as I wished I could plan my way through life, I couldn't stop tragedies, big or small, from happening. Even if I never set foot outside my comfort zone, sometimes life took a different, darker turn. And I realized that even when it did, I could adapt, I could cope. More than that, I could thrive. I resolved to make the most of now.

I had started the summer of my eighteenth year without a clue about what really mattered. It had taken a powerful shock to shake my perspective, and by the end of that summer, I was beginning to wake up.

Accidental Leaps

I couldn't have predicted that I would fall more than twenty feet from the wall of an indoor rock-climbing gym and smash my ankle and my leg—shattering all my plans and savings along with them. As much as we try to steer life, no one can ever know what's in store. But through experiences both unnerving and uplifting, I've learned to embrace both the excitement and fear in the unknown.

Freshly home from our trip to Europe, still riding the euphoric high of the Tomorrowland festival and questioning whether a nine-to-five job was for me, I'd started a new countdown: we'd go to Europe again next year. It wasn't a question—it was a declaration. The countdown signified it.

Michael's mom, Jan, had a countdown of her own. Every time I saw her, I'd ask for an update on her countdown.

"Seven years, nine months, and twenty-two days until retirement," she would singsong. "Not too much longer, and then I can do whatever I want."

But as the years passed and her health declined, she clung to that countdown like a lifeline . . . counting down the days until she could stop commuting to work, working for someone else, and simply do what she wanted—which mostly involved watching Lifetime movies and spending time with her Russian blue cat, Ivan, and her grandkids. She didn't have extravagant plans, but she wanted her life to be on her own terms. I admired that.

The risk we often overlook is waiting to pursue our dreams, pushing them off to a future that we hope will bring us closer to them. We make countdowns for the grand events in our futures, but we risk wasting our lives when we don't pursue now, today, what truly matters to us. A lesson I would soon learn.

Now back into the swing of normal life, I was thrilled that my favorite annual event was coming back: the State Fair of Texas. I'd don my stretchiest spandex leggings so I could try this year's fried-food concoctions (fried cookie dough, fried bacon, fried Coke—yes, really) and watch the pig races, play the midway games, and peruse the stands to shop. Magically-locking "As Seen on TV" Tupperware sat next to enormous cowhide rugs, which sat next to shoe polish, which sat next to a salsa-tasting stand, which sat next to Krazy Kruiser scooters. It was glorious. Dallas doesn't possess that down-home country feel that many cities in Texas offer, except when it comes to the fair.

"I am so excited for our Thanksgiving trip this year," I said, smiling as we watched a dog leap into the air and catch a Frisbee in the sawdust-covered arena.

"It will be nice. We have a lot coming up: Thanksgiving, Calvin and Kristina's wedding, Oktoberfest. Don't forget we have plans with my dad for dinner tonight," Michael reminded me.

After a Fletcher's corn dog lined with mustard that I inevitably spilled on my white T-shirt, I grabbed a bag of cotton candy as it started to rain.

From the fair we needed to get to a local rock-climbing gym for one of Michael's work events. He organized healthy activities for a hospital in Dallas, including outdoor walks, hikes, bike rides, and rock climbing. As we entered the gym, the familiar scent of sweat and chalk dust made my sugar-laden stomach turn. Recently, I'd used a Groupon to rock climb three days a week during a one-month membership at a local climbing gym. I was getting the hang of it, and I'd even started using terminology like "belaying" and creating a route as I climbed. But no one would threaten to call me a dirtbag (lingo for a rock climber who really knows what they're doing and probably doesn't use Groupon), and so far, I had only ever climbed with Michael.

Everyone in the group began to pair off, making small talk. While Michael went to help the novice climbers, I noticed a young woman without a partner, so I offered to pair with her.

She smiled and said softly, "Yeah, that'd be great."

After watching a short safety-demonstration video, a staff member briefed us on how to belay and answered questions to ensure we'd climb safely. As a class, we learned that the belay system—the rope, the anchors, the belay device itself, and the belayer who controls the ropes—uses the friction on the rope to help prevent falls. It's the most crucial safety mechanism for climbing.

"Okay, so, like, yeah, what you're going to do is, like, put your legs through the loops," he instructed.

His blond hair fell into his eyes every few seconds, and he had to keep flicking it away. I felt as if I were watching a young Justin Bieber give a safety demonstration. He must have been around sixteen, which—to my twenty-five-year-old self—made him seem like a small child.

My partner and I began climbing, trading off belaying. I felt buoyant from last month's experiences. I wasn't an expert, but I didn't fear heights. Rock climbing provided an uneasy rush, something that Michael loved, and I had grown stronger with each attempt. As a methodical adventure seeker, I felt that rock climbing was a nicely balanced calculated risk with its safety demonstrations, floor mats, and belay system.

Still feeling limber, I decided to do one last run. I headed up the thirty-foot wall, a bead of sweat snaking down the side of my face as I clenched the neon-colored handholds and got my footing. I carefully gripped the fake rocks, each one a different shape and size, feeling for the next hold that would take me higher.

Finally I reached the top, my limbs trembling. When I tugged gently on the rope, my stomach jolted: the rope was slack when it should be taut.

I waved my hands in the air. "Tension!" I called out.

My partner stared up at me momentarily before replying, "Gotcha!"

I inched down the wall about five feet.

"Helene," she said, "I got you."

I caught some slight annoyance in her tone, but I said anyway, just to confirm: "Okay, you have me?" I stared down from what must have been twenty-five feet or so up.

"I got you," she said. "You can come down."

I jumped back off the wall with all my might, throwing my weight into the harness as I'd done dozens of times before.

Right away something felt wrong. Frantically, I grasped at the air as I looked up to see the rope slipping quickly past the bar above me.

"LET GO!" I screamed as I was free-falling to the ground. "LET GO! LET GO!"

If she let go of the belay device, it would clamp shut, keeping me from falling.

But she just looked at me in shock, still holding the belay device open, her mouth open too as she watched me plummet toward the mats. The gray climbing wall and neon rocks flashed past as I hurtled to the bottom.

Crunch.

A sickening noise pierced my ears, and I looked in horror at my right leg, now twisted at an impossible angle, the bones shattered. The pain seared through my body like a white-hot flame.

In her own state of alarm, my partner started to run away from me, her face ashen with shock and terror. Then she realized she was still attached to me and my injured right leg, dragging me across the floor.

Michael rushed over, his jaw tense, a thunderstorm flashing in his eyes. He looked as if he were trying to calm himself down as he knelt beside me. "You'll be okay," he said, smoothing back my hair.

"I don't want to look at my leg," I whispered.

"You don't have to. You can just look at me."

I didn't cry. I sat there in shock. How had I not cracked my skull or paralyzed my back? I just kept focusing on Michael's eyes, which had now calmed from a thunderstorm to a drizzle. I wasn't okay, but I would be.

The next few hours were a blur of paramedics, an ambulance, and doctors. The hospital was a stark contrast to the chaos of the rock-climbing gym. The sterile smell of disinfectant lingered in the air, only the constant beeping of machines and the whispers of medical staff filling the silence.

I laughed and asked if they were going to write which ankle needed operating before they put me under for emergency surgery.

A stern-faced nurse carrying a Sharpie did not crack a smile as she wrote an X on my mangled leg.

Eight screws and a metal plate later, I woke up woozy in a hospital room, my leg throbbing with pain and my mind reeling from the shock of my new reality.

I spent the next five days in the hospital due to trouble breathing and a heightened heart rate. Then I caught pneumonia, adding to my already unbearable discomfort.

I kept trying to tell myself that things could have been way, way worse, but as I lay in my hospital bed, the unknown felt insurmountable. Would I still have a job? How would I get to work? Could we still go on the trip we'd planned over Thanksgiving? What about our friends' wedding? I felt as if my life were over.

And, in a way, it was. But not in the way I'd expected.

The Flashing of Hope

Since I can remember, I've been on the lookout for clues to what I should be doing with my life. In first grade I was Mary in the school play. Is this it? I asked the universe. Or, in this case, God. I remember looking out from center stage at the audience of parents, wondering if acting was my destiny.

I latched onto compliments quickly, searching for guidance in any praise. So when my second-grade teacher told me I could write, I unabashedly assumed I'd be a writer.

My parents were my only models for successful writers, but I had no desire to become a journalist like them. Still, when it was time to apply for college, I only applied to one: Southern Methodist University, where both of my parents were professors. I even tried out broadcast journalism my freshman year, only to shudder at the early mornings and copious amounts of makeup.

Then I tried out for the theater program, assuming I was a shoo-in since I'd acted all through grade and high school. It was the one thing I knew I was good at. But when I didn't get in, I decided theater wasn't for me either. I learned that I'm quick to give up on something at the first blush of failure.

When I graduated college in 2009, smack-dab in the middle of a financial crisis, the job market was scarce. Desperate for a sign, I saw one, a literal billboard: Texas needs teachers NOW! I signed up to get my teaching certificate the next day, then started taking substitute teaching jobs at all the Catholic schools around Dallas.

In between, I looked online for jobs.

"What do you want to do with your life?" my uncle Maney asked me. People love asking new college graduates this question, as if they can scan a QR code on your diploma and get the answer.

"I don't know," I said. "I'm trying to figure out if teaching is right for me."

"You don't want to teach children, Helene," he said, as if I were just not the type.

My uncle was a successful entrepreneur whose business rented out vending machines and trailers. "You just have to find it."

But what was this elusive it?

I found a job posting at my old grade school, St. Monica Catholic School, subbing for the kindergarten class. As I walked through the familiar halls, I took in the white linoleum floors, pale gray walls, and the scent of crayons. Memories came flooding back. I passed by the principal's office.

"Hello, Helene!" Mrs. Dulac, my math teacher turned principal, said. "It's great to see you."

Gray-haired and no-nonsense, she had occasionally ended up with dry-erase marker on her face during our math lessons.

"I'm nervous. I hope I do okay," I said, shaking her hand and looking up (which I often did at five feet two).

"You'll be great!" she assured me. "The kindergarten class is very sweet."

The bell rang, and I went inside the classroom. Low desks were arranged in circles on a brightly colored carpet. The instructions left on the teacher's desk told me to guide the students through writing their names on construction paper and cutting out a blue circle and an orange star around their names.

As I walked around the room, the kids worked, their tongues sticking out in concentration. One little boy kept turning away from me every time I passed by.

"How's it going, Matthew?" I asked, reading the name on his paper.

"Fine," he said, giving me a sideways glance and turning away again.

When it was time to turn in the assignment, Matthew approached the desk, wide-eyed. I noticed that his eyes looked even wider because he had just cut several inches of his long curly black hair right from the middle of his head.

He looked like a baby version of eighties Rod Stewart, his hair long on the sides with a tiny black plant sprouting on top. In the carpool line outside the school, I had to explain to Matthew's mother that I was responsible for his missing locks and the reason her son looked like he'd stuck his finger in an electrical outlet. My uncle was right: teaching wasn't for me.

So, again, after the first whiff of failure, I quit.

I'd been applying to jobs in marketing and PR while subbing, and later that week I heard back from Dave & Buster's corporate office in Dallas, Texas, about a promising position working in events. After a round of three interviews, one of which involved a test, I got the job. I was overjoyed, not because it was my dream job, but because I was barely able to pay my rent.

The salary wasn't anything amazing, but the perks were, to me, incredible. I got to eat, drink, and play for free at any Dave & Buster's in the country—and I could bring my friends along. When you're in your early twenties, getting to eat for free makes you feel invincible. If all else failed, I knew I wouldn't go hungry. Michael and I went at least twice a week. I'd order my favorite strawberry pecan chicken salad, then play Dance Dance Revolution before going home to our cozy 620-square-foot apartment.

My job entailed speaking with clients and peppering our conversations with lighthearted jokes. I prided myself on being the first to return calls, which led to quick promotions and opportunities to train others in a new sales system. Maybe this would be my ticket to travel, I thought.

But after visiting Denver, Chicago, and Philadelphia to see only the neon glow of Dave & Buster's signs, I knew this wasn't how I wanted to spend my days.

Yet there I was a year later, my leg propped up on a pile of pillows, working from our faux leather love seat for the foreseeable future after the rock-climbing accident.

It had been quite a year for us—getting married, buying a house, adopting a dog, and taking the trip of a lifetime. We'd started slowly saving in case we did move abroad, making a separate account called "the FUNd." But we kept finding reasons not to go.

Then everything had come crashing down—quite literally. But through all that pain, I'd noticed a new sense of clarity I hadn't had before. Stuck on our couch, I began to appreciate the little things more. I lost some sense of duty that so many of us feel like we have to subscribe to: trends, fashion, new cars and bigger houses and a smaller waist size. The innate force of consumerism seemed to lift its grasp on me when I started using a walker at age twenty-five.

I spent my time on the couch, watching *Friday Night Lights*, and when I wasn't doing that, I was spending every hour on the phone with medical billing. It would cost seven thousand dollars out of pocket for my surgery. There went the money we'd been saving to move abroad.

Real life had smacked me in the face. Or, in this case, the ankle.

I'd spent so many years in a frenzied state searching for how to balance a happy marriage, homeownership, a career, while also trying to make more money for all the things Michael and I wanted to do. I was worried that life was passing me by, that the clock was ticking. But suddenly this fall had jolted me out of my routine. And I realized that I wasn't actually thinking about what I truly wanted out of life.

Now that I'd really started to consider what a fulfilling life could look like, I was desperate to get off that couch. So I searched "broken ankle recovery time" on Google. After scrolling through medical journals, news sources, and WebMD articles, I stumbled upon a blog written by a woman about my age who was talking about her ankle injury in a funny and relatable way. I spent the whole day reading her website and, as I clicked through her archives, it dawned on me: I could start my own blog.

I didn't start the blog to make money. I simply wanted an outlet to talk about my broken ankle, my obsessions (mainly Diet Coke, Britney Spears, and *The Bachelor* recaps), what I thought were the good old days as a senior in high school, and past travels. I never forgot my second-grade teacher telling me I could write.

What do I really want to do with my life? I thought. Where will I want to be, live, work in five or even fifteen years? I'd always felt I was somewhere "in between," one foot here and the other planted there. Something clicked, and I knew that this name was the one for my blog: Helene in Between. It even rhymed.

I joined blogging groups, maintained a regular posting schedule, and found a community. I wasn't making a single penny, but I felt compelled to share. I even connected with others who had also broken their ankles. I found solace in talking with people who could relate, and they helped me make sense of my experiences. Whole days would go by when I completely forgot about my misery, and the pain in my ankle seemed to dissipate whenever I logged in to my blog.

"Now this would be a cool job," I told my Doberman, Hugo, who was snoozing by my injured leg, protecting it. But that wasn't possible. That was for real websites like Cupcakes & Cashmere for the fashion and cute hairstyles, or Rick Steves—the authority on European travel.

I found that I gravitated to the performance aspect of writing on the internet: receiving immediate feedback from others watching my life. Maybe I could find my way back to the stage in a different way.

My blog became my glimmer of hope. The flashing cursor might as well have been a comforting hand tapping me on the shoulder: There's more out there—go find it. I'd found a way to connect with others, to share my struggles and triumphs, and to explore the possibilities of what else I could do with my life.

But where could this lead me?

An Entire Country
Observing a Nap

After six months in physical therapy, my ankle nearly recovered, I finally hobbled back to the office and plunked myself down at my desk. I could feel my focus waning. So I opened my browser and googled "how to move abroad."

Images of lean, tan couples carrying all their belongings on their backs in Bali flashed on the screen. Guys with man buns and suspiciously toned six-pack abs threw their heads back in laughter as they gripped fixed-gear bike handles. Women in gauzy white tops perched over foamy lattes and laptops while waves crashed and palm trees swayed in the background.

"Follow that Dream" floated on a sign next to the beautiful people. It seemed nice—serene, even—until I thought of the one time I'd tried to work outside on our deck on a summer day. Beads of sweat had trickled into my eyes as I shifted in my seat over and over, trying in vain to shield my laptop screen from the sun. How could anyone get any work done with all that glare?

Then I started reading some stories about people who'd lived abroad after joining the military and others whose companies had sent them overseas on a temporary assignment. But I couldn't see myself in any of them. Where were all the normal people? Did you really have to shirk all responsibility to find adventure in a foreign country? We couldn't do that. What about our mortgage and our dog's heart, flea, and tick medication? Plus, Michael couldn't pull off a man bun.

I wanted to move abroad. I wanted to gaze under the glittering Eiffel Tower on a Tuesday evening or have an impromptu picnic on the River Seine. But I had too much at stake to throw it all away. I needed that stability to function. I didn't own any white gauzy tops anyway.

Then one blog in particular caught my attention—aha. This writer had met a Spaniard abroad, gotten married, and moved to Spain with him. Now I was inspired. Okay, not to run off and marry a Spaniard, but to go to Spain. I furiously started making a list of museums, sights, restaurants . . .

And that was when my manager came up behind me.

"Is this"—she paused—"work?"

Usually, I was pretty good at making up excuses on the spot, but the pixelated images of Sagrada Familia were hard to explain away.

Busted.

"No, sorry," I responded, and clicked back to the bright orange-and-blue Dave & Buster's logo on my home screen.

Maybe I couldn't move to Spain. Maybe I couldn't move abroad, but maybe, just maybe, I could get a raise. As soon as I stopped getting caught planning trips during work hours, of course. More money would solve my problems. Not long after, I summoned the courage, brought along a manila folder full of accolades, and wore my only pair of high heels paired with a smart black pencil skirt and white button-up blouse . . . and asked my boss for a raise.

I didn't get it. So after three and a half years at Dave and Buster's, I knew it was time to go.

I took a digital marketing and SEO position thirty-five minutes farther north of home. First step: google "SEO," or "search engine optimization." The first six months on the job were all training: SEO, pay-per-click (PPC) advertising, social media advertising, website design and development, and lead generation. Then finally I was assigned a salesperson. My job was to help create and implement ads and social media that the salesperson sold. My guy lived in New York and he was always, always furious with me—probably because I wasn't good at the job, or maybe he was just uptight, or maybe it was a little of both. We'll never know for sure because I never met him in person, but based on how often he'd berate me because Plumber John's ads weren't on the first page of Google's search results yet, I imagined he wore a too-tight gray suit and had a buzz cut and a standing reservation at Dorsia. He'd fit in with the businessmen in *American Psycho.*

On Fridays, we had company-wide meetings that my boss's boss, Caleb Leer, would oversee. At the end of the meeting, he'd read anonymous messages from "Leer's Box." Who knows which suck-up put these messages in the box, but they were overwhelmingly kind and positive. There might have even been a "You have the best hair, Leer!"

Leer always ended meetings with "Love you guys." I was pretty sure the man didn't even know my first name.

I officially hated my job. During lunch breaks, I self-medicated with junk food: Chick-fil-A or Target. The drives home were maddening too: an hour in bumper-to-bumper traffic one disheartening day after another. Staring at brake lights through a tinted windshield, I felt rage bubble up inside me. I'd come home angry and sad, feeling as if I'd wasted another day of my twenties at a meaningless job, then sitting in never-ending traffic. Did everyone feel this way?

Was it just a rite of passage to hate your job? Certainly, there had to be more to life.

"Let's go to Spain," I said to Michael through gritted teeth, slamming the garage door behind me.

As soon as I could walk without help again, Michael, Josh, and I planned another trip to Europe, this time to Barcelona, Ibiza, and Madrid.

With my name corrected on my passport, traveling to Europe was smooth sailing. During our three days in Barcelona, we saw the still-under-construction Sagrada Familia, Parc Güell, and the Picasso Museum.

The wide, bustling boulevards of Barcelona were filled with galleries, restaurants, and shops until they met the sand. Locals and tourists stretched out on towels like lizards in the sun along the three miles of coastline. I was enthralled with the Gaudí architecture, particularly Casa Batlló, with its iridescent dragon scales snaking up the building and skull-and-bone balconies.

Weary from walking through Parc Güell and standing for hours at the Picasso Museum, we searched for an open café. We passed by darkened café windows along the busy street, La Rambla.

I squinted at a handwritten cardboard sign: Respeten el horario de siesta de 4 a 7 a de la tarde. Even with my limited Spanish, I was able to decipher enough: "Respect the siesta schedule from 4 to 7 in the afternoon." We'd forgotten about siesta. Spaniards often follow the tradition of taking a two- or three-hour break in the heat of the day to rest and catch up with family. Whoops. We had not prepared for this.

Stomachs growling, we spotted an open gelato shop and we each ordered two scoops on waffle cones. We ate our quickly melting treats as we sat on green benches overlooking la Plaça de Catalunya, a huge square whose holm oak trees cast a mosaic of sunlight on the ground. I picked up a Wi-Fi signal from a nearby hotel and googled "Spanish siesta."

"Okay, apparently this is a thing," I said, raising my finger and reading from my screen. "'The siesta is believed to have originated in Ancient Rome but became popular in Spain during the Spanish Civil War. According to one popular theory, its purpose was to give field workers a break during the hottest hours of the day.'"

"Can you even imagine?" Michael mused, biting into his waffle cone. "A whole country observing a nap."

"That's what I love about Europe," I said, tucking my phone back in my purse. "They're still happily entrenched in the old-world ways. It still even looks mostly the same."

We were the first to arrive when restaurants opened back up for dinner, waiting at a door before the neon sign had even been turned back on.

Ibiza flew by in a flash: a dingy hostel with a miniscule pink-tiled bathroom, fresh paella, luxurious sea breezes, and quiet cream-colored sandy beaches. We went to clubs every night, which felt like different worlds entirely from the bright, serene coastline we saw by day.

On our final day, we decided to have one last celebratory dinner at ten o'clock.

"You'll need to finish by midnight, as we have a reservation at that time," the hostess announced, showing us to our table.

"That should be no problem," I assured her, but figured I'd misheard her. Dinner at midnight? Yeah, right.

But sure enough, at midnight a family of five strolled over to our table, the little kids bursting with energy for their midnight dinner. Our mouths hung open. Maybe an afternoon nap was the way to go after all.

We concluded our trip in Madrid, where we marveled at masterpieces in the Museo Nacional del Prado, took a day trip to the ancient aqueducts of Segovia, and let the solemn beauty of the churches wash over us. On our last night, we went to a flamenco show held in a small, intimate room with wicker chairs tightly packed around six or seven wooden tables. Under dim light, the audience spoke in hushed, reverent voices, the hum of the fans the only sound before the show began.

The musicians silently took their place onstage, the women with their hair in low, slicked-back ponytails, the men carrying guitars. Two men and two women took turns performing solo dances. Their performances were so personal and evocative that we could almost grasp the emotional charge of each movement. It was unlike any live theater or show I'd ever seen. One woman soloist, in particular, moved me to tears. She wore a traditional flamenco dress: a long, purple velvet gown that clung to her body, with long fringe tassels cinching at the knees, paired with a gold floral vest. She pounded and stamped so hard on the wooden stage that a floorboard chipped, soaring into the audience.

After the show, we walked home silently, letting the sounds of Madrid's streets fill the air. I slowed my own thoughts to find myself in the present moment, taking in, feeling what we'd just beheld. I felt my fingertips tingle in the soft breeze and the bottoms of my feet spring against the sturdy, ancient cobblestones. I felt held by those streets as old as civilization, and I could only wonder, Will I ever do something that I care that much about?

I couldn't envision myself living in Spain, but the pull of Europe felt overwhelming. Were they living life better here? Or was I just stuck in my own rut of traffic and brake lights and uninspiring jobs?

A Baby Cold

My friends were starting to think about having children. I was planning a trip to Greece. Travel and children aren't mutually exclusive, but I had a nagging feeling that maybe raising kids wasn't for me.

Michael and I both grew up Catholic. His parents, especially his mother, were staunch Catholics. My parents aren't staunch about anything—religion, politics, sports—except about hailing from Louisiana. They are staunchly from Louisiana. But having kids is integral to Catholicism. Many staunch Catholics, like Michael's mom, don't believe in birth control and feel it's a sin to try not to have kids.

I'd always thought we would. Michael and I wrote each other sappy letters during our long-distance relationship in college, often talking about how one day we would start a family together. I felt bad for not wanting kids. Was something wrong with me?

It seemed so, yes. I posted on my blog that I had a "baby cold," meaning the opposite of baby fever: I didn't think kids were for me. Traffic had been starting to trickle in to my blog and some of my posts were being discovered on Google (thanks, terrible SEO job!), but this was different. Hundreds of comments poured in.

To my own surprise, I found that I was able to be honest—even with vulnerable topics—more so on my blog than in my day-to-day life.

It seemed like everyone around me (friends, bloggers, etc.) wanted to have a baby, get pregnant, or had a kid already. I was—and am—FAR from that. I don't know if it's selfishness, immaturity, or plainly a lack of the motherly gene, but I know that I don't want them. At least for now. And here's a problem (judge away): I like being the center of attention. I know, I know. That's bad. But I do. I like that my husband focuses on me, rather than a child who needs constant attention.

At that point, I had never confronted my own true reasons for not wanting kids. Michael and I had only nodded in agreement and said "not now." At twenty-six—which may as well be thirty-eight in Texas—people were wondering why we weren't entertaining the idea.

We put off the decision by getting another dog instead. Millie was the cutest English springer spaniel I'd ever seen. Now I didn't have to figure out whether or not I really wanted kids, at least not anytime soon. No Catholic guilt for me!

Being seven years older than my twin sisters, I've often felt like a pseudo-parent. I was not the cool older sibling. I did not buy them beer. In fact, when my parents went out of town, I'd ground them for talking back to me. I don't think they are over that. It's okay—neither am I.

I had babysitting jobs when I was a teenager, and I'd always liked kids. But my favorite jobs were watching the older kids, who went to bed easily on their own. After they were asleep I'd raid the kitchen and eat their Trix yogurt and Dunkaroos and turn on *The Bachelor*. I noticed that all of the contestants on that show really seemed to want to have kids, like yesterday.

The internet was horrified by my post.

You'll change your mind.

You'll never know true love if you don't have kids.

You'll miss out on one of life's greatest and most fulfilling experiences.

Whoa. Well, you are too, I thought. Because we were attending the Tomorrowland music festival for the third time, then going to Greece and Prague. Couldn't this trip also be one of life's greatest experiences?

Better travel now—before you have kids, others chimed.

Because no way was it possible that maybe, just maybe, I wouldn't have kids at all.

But the worst comment was this one: You'll regret it. That one stung, but I thought, what if I had kids, then regretted having them? That seemed far worse.

No one commented that I might regret not going to Greece or moving abroad or starting a business. But not bringing a human into this world? That would be a regret.

Could I have a fulfilled life—as a whole person—without a baby? I didn't know. But I packed my bags, tucked away the worry, and pulled out my passport instead. Maybe my life could be different, and that would be okay. Maybe I would take a different sort of leap instead.

All I knew about Greece had come from watching the play *Mamma Mia!* in London. It felt wistful and romantic. Would locals sing to us in the streets? Would restaurant staff erupt into a dance number before dinner?

As soon as we touched down in Athens, I felt a renewed sense of peace and exhilaration, as if I were embarking inside a story already being told. But as I took the escalator up to leave the airport, I felt someone behind me attempting to unzip my backpack. I turned around before a well-dressed, middle-aged man was able to steal anything. I looked at him and shook my head, and he darted off. Honestly, the most he could have snagged was a light-up flower crown, socks, and a beat-up iPhone charger. I'd been warned, like every American, about pickpocketing in Europe, and I took this close call as a reminder to be careful and present. But I wasn't deterred in the slightest.

We set out for dinner after dropping our bags at the hotel. We found a dimly lit outdoor café near the Acropolis. The setting sun cast a dazzling copper glow over everything in sight.

Our waiter introduced himself as "Christmas," and he chuckled after every few words as if he were training to become Santa Claus. I already loved Greece. Christmas brought out chilled red wine in a carafe and crisp Greek salads. As we were getting up to leave, he took a picture of us and told us "Siga, siga," which meant to slow down, to take your time. Too late. We were packing as much into this trip as possible.

The next day, we got up early for a full day: the Acropolis Museum, Zeus's temple, and the Athens National Garden.

With thousands of others, we climbed the hill to the Acropolis, and as we came closer and closer, we were shocked to see how truly enormous the Parthenon was. The complex where the Greeks had worshiped Athena still remained sacred centuries later.

The next day, we set off to Santorini by ferry, where we stayed at Hotel Perissa for €45 a night. When we docked, Freddy, the hotel owner, sent a driver to pick us up. We ate greasy kebabs and ventured to a local bar. We stayed up until we could feel our eyelids prick with delirium. And when I finally made it to bed, that nagging question tugged at me as I pulled up the sheets. I knew that having kids wouldn't necessarily preclude me from living a life of adventure. Maybe it would be more challenging, sure. But the real question was: Did I actually want them? Or did I feel I needed to have kids because that's what everyone else was doing?

I pushed the thought aside and crawled into the tiny, firm bed with a lumpy pillow. I slept deeply for about five hours. I was in Santorini for crying out loud!

When we woke up the next morning, we were greeted with gorgeous views of the cliffs beyond, a pebble-lined swimming pool just below, and grapes growing by the side of the road.

We drove around the island, laughing and singing, feeling as light as the feathery trees swaying in the wind. Blue-and-white flags fluttered proudly as the sun baked the dusty pavement. Crisp white buildings with azure-colored dome roofs clung to the cliffs, seeming to pile on top of each other as they snaked their way to the end of the island.

We ventured into the crowded towns of Oia and Fira, but our favorite places were the quieter, less touristy spots: abandoned churches perched on hilltops, the stark white paint withering away to gray. I could easily imagine living a simple life on the island of Santorini. Eating yogurt, drinking wine, and living in a tiny white house.

Our trip passed too quickly, and we hopped on another ferry, this time to Crete, heading straight to Preveli Beach, where crystal-clear river water met the sea. It was nothing like I'd ever seen before. As we drove through the maze of tiny streets winding along the rocky cliffs, I stuck my head out the window, hair blowing, my skin wet from jumping in the Libyan Sea, singing *Mamma Mia!* songs. I felt as free as the breeze against my skin.

We took a short plane ride from Crete to Prague, and it was as if we'd landed in a completely different world. The city was full of gorgeous ornate buildings clustered close to one another. We took a tram through the city, gazing at the twinkling lights of Prague Castle.

We walked along Charles Bridge, taking pictures of every statue and rubbing the stone dog for good luck. We marveled at the elaborate St. Vitus Cathedral. We strolled and shopped at the Golden Lane. We walked more miles than we'd ever walked before on a trip.

On the plane ride home, I sat next to a talkative man wearing a wide-brimmed, waterproof hat fastened at his chin, as if a sudden gust of wind might blow or we might happen upon a lion on safari. I was sleepy and had work the next day, but I was eager to talk to anyone about our trip.

"So, what do you have planned next?" he asked as the flight attendant handed us pretzels.

Before I could answer, he said, "Kids?" He nodded at Michael, who was wearing headphones and had missed the man's question.

"Oh, um, no, not yet," I said, blushing.

"You're young—you have time," he continued. "Where to next?"

"I don't know." I fumbled with my wedding ring, feeling more put on the spot than the question warranted. "Maybe Scotland."

"Oh! Yes, you must go," the man with the hat said wistfully. "That was my first trip to Europe. And this was my first trip back here in thirty years." He finally took off his hat, as if in reverence.

He continued to tell me about his jaunt across the Scottish Highlands, how mesmerized he was by the green countryside, the hairy Highland coos, the mystical lochs. "I'd always hoped to go back, even move there. Maybe one day I will."

As I listened to his story, I realized that I didn't just want to hope that one day I'd make my own dreams of living abroad happen. I wanted to do it now. I couldn't live with having only a few trips to savor. I wanted a life filled to the brim with these memories.

So many of us hold on to only a handful of travel memories, often defining parts of ourselves by them. We carry these vivid, transformative experiences with us for the rest of our lives—souvenirs, gauzy snapshots we turn to again and again.

The man's question about kids, innocent enough, stayed with me long after I got off the plane. I didn't know whether I could live a happy life without procreating, but I knew that I'd regret not living a life full of travel. And that's the question I should have been asking myself: not about whether I should have kids, but what was it that I couldn't live without? And there the answer was, staring out at me through the window, past that ridiculous wide-brimmed hat.

Losing the Dream

My parents ruined jobs for me. They love what they do, and they have no intention of ever retiring. They are writers, and they've both worked as journalists and professors. They've gotten awards for things they've done. They have flexible schedules. They somehow figured out how to get paid for their passion. It's sickening.

So when I started working a traditional nine-to-five, I was confused. Why must I endure these relentless meetings, busywork, and a commute in gridlocked traffic?

"Helene," Michael said one day after I came home and slammed the door—hard. "Most people don't have jobs like your parents."

But not only did I not like my job, I didn't know what to do with my life. I scrolled Facebook and saw posts from friends and acquaintances about getting promotions. But I didn't want to be a manager. A dentist. A broadcast journalist.

For me, the trouble with every job, ever, was that I had to work for someone else.

In college, I started a dance camp. I held it at my old middle school and made five thousand dollars in two months. This also ruined jobs for me because it made me think that I could do what I thought was fun and get paid. But earning five thousand dollars every summer wouldn't be enough to get me through life.

I was willing to work hard. That wasn't it. It's just that I wanted to do what I wanted and when I wanted to do it. And I really wanted to spend time with my dogs.

Breaking my ankle and leg further ruined jobs for me. When I couldn't drive, I worked from home for months, snuggling beside Hugo as he snoozed noisily. Somehow, being bed-bound and blacking out when I stood up too quickly was better than spending days under buzzing fluorescent lights in my cubicle, I knew things really had to change.

As many millennials do, I contemplated how I could make money on the side doing something I was passionate about. I tried as hard as I could to figure out a side hustle, even though I loathed this term. It always conjured to mind visions of peddling drugs and disco dance moves from the seventies.

For the first few years out of college, I tried my hand at countless side hustles—selling maroon knockoff jewelry to the devoted football fans at Texas A&M, hustling cheese samples at Kroger, making candles out of severed wine bottles—but none of my side hustles made any real money. Then I started a blog called *Do Dallas Cheap*. I'd wake up at five a.m. and scour deals-of-the-day sites like Groupon to compile the best deals before I got to work. I was exhausted. And no one was even reading the blog.

Every day I'd see quotes on social media about the importance of following your dreams, that you'd regret settling for helping someone else build theirs. I didn't completely prescribe to that thinking: being an employee can be satisfying, liberating, and often, when you pack up and leave the office, you're done for the day. There's tremendous value in that. I just knew it wasn't for me.

Then, one day, after working for Dave & Buster's, then selling ad space on Google, then doing social media for restaurants—I found it: my dream job. This was it, and I was jaded no longer. I'd just needed the right job.

And it had been hidden in plain sight: "Travel Communications Specialist for Southwest Airlines In-Flight Magazine."

The idea of writing for the magazine of an airline I knew and loved sounded almost too good to be true.

I read the description quickly, eager to get started on my application. As I kept reading, I got more and more excited. Applicants need to demonstrate the ability to remain calm under pressure, think quickly on their feet, and show a commitment to delivering exceptional and informative travel pieces. These content initiatives will focus on the travel realm and be featured in Southwest Airlines's in-flight magazine, both online and in print. Will include travel.

I applied immediately.

I got a standard reply back a few minutes later: Thank you for your interest. If your qualifications meet our needs, we will contact you for a possible interview. Due to the volume of résumés received, we request that applicants not call regarding submitted résumés. My heart sank. Maybe my application wouldn't shine through.

But two weeks later I got an email asking if I could send over some writing samples. Could I ever! I was a walking writing sample. I submitted my entire blog, pieces I'd published for other news outlets, and even a short article I'd written for my university's paper. Just in case.

I got an interview!

The first interview was conducted over the phone, and the interviewer asked me about my writing skills, what I enjoyed writing about, and my previous travels. I thought it went well.

Later that day I received a lengthy email informing me that the next step was a writing test and back-to-back interviews with three members of their team, all on the same day.

The writing exercise was up first. They asked me to pick a destination that the airline flew to and write a one-page sample for that city. I chose Austin, Texas, a city I was familiar with but felt could benefit from exposure to other aspects of its culture, since most people only knew about partying downtown on Sixth Street. I spent the evening carefully crafting the perfect destination and designed it exactly as the airline's magazine aligned their travel pages.

I submitted my writing sample and waited for the next interviews.

The day was long and stressful. Despite the individual interviews, each interviewer asked me nearly the same questions. The final interview was with a tall man wearing a blue-and-red-striped tie.

"Come on in," he said, ushering me into his office and sitting on a stool. "I see you have a little blog, how wonderful."

I sat opposite him, on a slightly lower stool, and nodded, unsure how to make up for my blog being "little."

"Yes," I replied sheepishly. "It's had over 3.5 million hits. Er, page views."

I felt stupid saying the ".5" and wished I'd just said "over three million," but he kept going.

"Great! This is a big magazine and a big job." He put his pointer finger to his lips and nodded.

Was this not a job I could do after working on such a "little" blog? I suddenly felt as if I had cotton in my ears. Like I couldn't quite pay attention to what this man was saying. I thought about our plans to move abroad, away from this tiny, stuffy office in Dallas.

"You know?" he asked, and I snapped back to reality.

But I did not know. Because I wasn't paying attention. I had been too focused on being too small.

"Your writing is good, really good. But we are looking for great."

"I believe I can be great if you'd give me the chance," I replied, straightening up on my stool.

He smiled, but it didn't quite reach his eyes.

The next day, I got an email from the man with the striped tie. He wrote, Cool, you have a blog—but can you really write? He then asked if I'd come in for one more interview.

This time I sat down with a young woman from HR whom I hadn't met yet and again the man with the striped tie, although today's tie was a solid navy. This was a good sign, right? I was clinging to whatever I could.

We sat informally in a circle, my legs crossed in my chunky black one-inch heels and calf-length black dress.

"Why do you want this job?" the man asked.

I was ready with an answer. "I think in-flight magazines are the last stronghold of print communication. You have the rapt attention of frequent flyers as well as those just taking a trip. It's the perfect opportunity to share things they might not know about or give them information about what they can learn along the way. I want to be their guide."

I saw the HR lady make a check mark on her clipboard. She smiled up at me and winked. I was excited—a new adventure was about to begin. The job was as good as mine.

Later that day I got an email from the HR woman: I'm sorry to inform you that we're going with someone else.

Six rounds of interviews and an encouraging wink from the HR lady and I still hadn't gotten the job. It felt like I was losing a dream. I called my dad.

"Ask them why," he said. "It will be good feedback to understand why you weren't the right fit. And maybe you should just keep the job you have now. You've jumped around an awful lot."

He was right. I had. This would be my third job in three years.

When I asked, HR responded via email: You are an extremely bright, talented professional. I know you will find a fantastic opportunity that fits you perfectly! But with a magazine at the core of what we do, we had to make sure we had someone with a really strong journalistic background in the role.

I was devastated. This was it. This had been my dream job and it had slipped through my fingers.

Maybe Michael was right: Maybe work wasn't supposed to be fun. Maybe everyone else hated their jobs and my parents were just lucky.

What I didn't realize was that not getting that job led me to finding the job that would change my life.

Fired in Nashville

Each year, Dallas throws a St. Patrick's Day parade on Greenville Avenue. Snoop Dogg was master of ceremonies one year. So, although it was no match for the celebrations in Ireland, the whole city came out in droves of green, slinging beer.

We'd all pile into a friend of a friend of a friend's house who lived in the neighborhood, don green, and drink too much as we walked from bar to bar.

The neighborhoods surrounding the parade were filled with expensive, beautiful homes with nearly no backyards and huge, grand indoor spaces for entertaining.

For this year's parade, Michael's coworker's friend invited us to a house in the neighborhood, though we had no idea who the owners were. We kept to the backyard, playing drinking games. At one point I wandered inside to use the restroom, only to find a long line snaking down the hallway. As I waited, I studied the paintings on the wall.

Clearly, this was someone's parents' house—no way a kid our age had an art collection like this. I noticed some photos of a happy family from the early nineties—three boys and two girls with their parents, all dressed in the same patterned gingham. My eyes landed on the painting next to it, of a blue-and-white domed village spilling out over a sapphire sea. I peered closer to get a look at the signature.

"Like that one?"

I whipped around.

"Yes, it's beautiful. Do you know where it was taken?" I asked, thinking it must be Greece but wanting to make sure.

A young woman about my age came closer, her Chanel earrings dangling. "Yeah, that's Santorini, in Greece. It's my dad's bucket-list place. He always wanted to go but never made the time. It's too far anyway. I think you have to take two flights and a ferry to get over there. Plus, you can get good Greek food around here."

"I've been," I said, smiling, cocking my head and looking closer at the painting. "It really wasn't that hard to get to. And it's absolutely stunning, the whole place—"

But she had already turned back around, apparently uninterested in my story.

Here I was in a gorgeous multimillion-dollar house in Dallas. And even though I had nowhere near the amount of money it would take to own a house like this one, I'd been to a place this woman's father had only ever dreamed of visiting. He'd dreamed of it so much that he'd hung a painting of it on his wall. Yet he never took the steps to get there. How was that possible?

Time stood still in the dark wood-paneled hallway. I walked outside and tore Michael away from his losing game of flip cup.

"Michael," I said, looking him straight in the eye. "We need to move abroad."

My words were desperate, but I knew he understood.

"I know," he replied. "We will. We just have to figure out how."

The answer, we thought, was through work.

For a long time I knew that I liked writing and I liked traveling and I wanted to combine the two. But it seemed as if the only people getting paid to do both of those things were working at publications like Lonely Planet. I realize now that I wouldn't have wanted to work at a place like that—because I didn't actually like writing when I had to write for someone else.

In 2015, I landed a remote position with a renowned marketing company. Its list of Fortune 500 clients was impressive, but I was more enthusiastic that my commute was a walk from one room to another.

With one remote job under our belts, Michael and I decided to get serious about moving abroad. My dad, who'd had prostate cancer and stage 3 melanoma, was now in remission, and Michael's mom's cancer was also at bay. With those clean bills of health, we felt like we could make a move.

As a first step, we decided to move to Nashville. It would be a huge change, since I'd never lived anywhere else but Dallas, Texas. Even my zip code had hardly changed in all twenty-eight years of my life. So before we took the real plunge and moved across the world, I wanted to make sure: Could we do this?

Michael was able to convince his boss to let him work remotely, and we made the ten-hour trek with Hugo, Millie, and all our stuff north to Nashville. Before we left, Michael's mom gave me a wooden box with my name inscribed on the top. Inside were all her favorite recipes, handwritten on note cards.

"I had a lot of time during my chemo treatments to do this," she said, running her fingers through her short hair, which was finally growing back.

My mom and dad also gave me a gift: a binder full of all the cards and notes they'd written me over the years. Each time they wrote me a letter on my birthday or during a momentous occasion, they'd kept a copy. These gifts gave me the final seal of approval that we were making the right decision.

With each passing state line, I felt questions bubble up and my stomach tighten. I was unsure about everything: renting out our home, my job, Michael's job, the health of our parents, where we would be living, my friends, my family . . . Would we lose more than we'd gain in moving away from it all? But the farther we drove, the more solidified I became in the decision. And I had to at least try to see what life would look like far away from everything I knew.

As we crossed the bridge from Arkansas to Tennessee, I felt a thrill of fear mixed with courage. I was casting off the shackles of what life was supposed to be like and opening myself willingly to the unknown. Hugo peered out the window, smudging the glass with his long, wet nose, the rolling green hills beckoning. For as long as I'd been alive, this was the most daring adventure I'd ever embarked on.

In Nashville, we spent our days working from home and our nights researching where to move abroad in Europe. Every Thursday and Sunday, we'd have a meeting in Michael's office. He'd sit at his desk and I'd bring in my laptop and sit on top of the blue duvet on the bed and we'd discuss our next move. I looked at my softball-sized globe and spun it: Where in the world should we live?

The plan was to move in the summer of 2016, exactly a year from our move to Nashville.

On the weekends, we explored our new city. We tried a new hot chicken restaurant and ate at hole-in-the-wall barbecue joints. We attended festivals and county fairs. We were having a blast. Michael's college friend lived in Nashville, and he and his girlfriend had swept us up into their friend group as if we, too, had been born and raised there. We didn't stress over making new friends, and life felt pretty good, even away from home.

I began to work more on my blog. One of my first major events was a live workshop for my budding audience on how to grow an online following.

But meanwhile, I hated my actual job and had started shirking my responsibilities. I got a few reprimands saying that the emails I was sending out to clients weren't up to company standards, but I pushed them aside.

On the day of the live course, I was a ball of nerves and excitement. I looked over my PowerPoint and decided that I'd send my 2,023 email subscribers one final push to sign up for the workshop.

I carefully read and reread the email I was about to send (probably more carefully than I read the emails I was sending for work). As my cursor hovered over "send," I noticed an email pop up—it was from my boss.

The subject line read, Confirmation of employment termination. Whoa. Apparently, I had failed to meet performance requirements for the last time. Specifically, I'd sent today's email with an Oxford comma.

Well, that was it. I was fired over an Oxford comma. I was shocked and confused. But oddly, I wasn't devastated.

I shut down my computer and walked outside. Was I dreaming? Maybe I needed a system reboot.

Because I was not this person. I did not get fired. And I certainly didn't get fired over an Oxford comma. But as the hot September air grazed my skin, I felt a sense of calm. I walked around barefoot in our tiny yard in Nashville, Millie and Hugo staring at me, heads cocked. I sat down on the grass and looked them each in the eye.

"I'll figure it out," I told them.

I reread the email from my boss. I was fired, for real. Now tonight's workshop would be pivotal. And more than that, it was a chance to prove that I could do this—work for myself.

Michael got home an hour before the workshop.

"Let's run through everything, make sure it goes smoothly as soon as you go live," he offered.

He sat in his office, watching on his computer as I did a mini run-through on mine. He knocked on the wall separating our rooms and called out, "I can see you. All looks good!"

"Okay, and you can hear me?"

"Yep, all clear," he yelled.

"Well, I have something to tell you, and I don't have time to discuss it now." I gulped, looking into my own eyes on the computer screen. Michael didn't reply, so I went on.

"I got fired today."

I could hear his computer chair squeak. "What?" he said, now standing in the doorway.

"I know." I turned, looking down at my hands in my lap. "They said they warned me before, and I used an Oxford comma in an email to a client . . ."

"Okay, we can talk about this later, but right now you need to focus on the workshop. And it sounds like you need to do a pretty good job."

I splashed water on my face and reapplied my makeup. Then, at seven p.m. Central Time, on the dot, I sat in my chair and clicked the flashing red button to go live. I was stepping onstage and into an unfamiliar spotlight, but as I got into a rhythm—speaking to dozens of eager faces as they looked back at my own—I knew this was right. The attendees were engaged, they asked insightful questions, and I felt as if I were floating on air throughout the entire two-hour workshop. I was doing something valuable. Something helpful.

At the end of the workshop, I called downstairs to Michael, who rushed in.

"Well . . . how'd it go?"

"It went off without a hitch!" I squealed.

"And how many sales did you end up getting?"

"I honestly don't know." I turned to face my laptop. "Let's find out."

I opened up my sales page and quickly looked at the total. Before saying it out loud, I calculated it again to make sure it was correct.

"Eight thousand dollars," I said, my mouth suddenly dry and my eyes unfocused.

"What?" Michael screamed. "Seriously? Oh my god."

I looked back at the figure. "Yes. $8,162 total."

"Wow," Michael said. "Now that is something."

Lantern Wishes

Michael wandered into my office at midnight holding a popsicle. "Are you going to go to bed soon?" he asked.

I'd found my passion for blogging again, often losing my sense of time in the process, and it had begun to pay off. My work geared toward aspiring content creators was taking off, and my second course had earned more than the first. Other followers had started writing thank-you notes to me, grateful for the travel itineraries and product recommendations. I'd found that spark again, and—inundated with ideas—I just couldn't type fast enough. It seemed that once I'd decided to change my life, the pieces were falling into place more quickly than I could catch them.

And here was my plan: give myself nine months to grow my blog and social media presence before we moved abroad.

One question loomed: Was it sustainable? I hoped I could keep the momentum going.

"I guess you should work now. Not sure how good the signal will be in Asia," Michael mumbled, chewing his popsicle. Such an odd way to eat a popsicle. "And we still need to decide where we're moving."

"Who chews popsicles?" I retorted, shelving the weight of his statement. It was past midnight, after all. Major life decisions could wait.

Over the past few months, we'd narrowed down our potential new home to Germany—so far. We'd traveled to and ruled out London, Amsterdam, Prague, Barcelona, and Paris, but there were still other cities on our list. It was wild to think we would move to a place we'd never been to before.

"Florence has the most gorgeous architecture I've ever seen . . . and we could eat gelato all the time," I said, sighing as I looked at a photo of the red-tiled cupola of the Duomo and the maze of streets beneath it.

"Yeah, but we might have to learn Italian." Michael picked at the hairs of his mustache. "Brussels could be cool. Then we could easily go to Tomorrowland every year. Or we could move to Prague. I'd look like the locals." Both sides of Michael's family were from Czechia—formerly known as the Czech Republic—and during our trip in 2013 he kept remarking how much he fit in—at least aesthetically.

I rolled my eyes.

Germany kept popping up on the "best of" lists and online quizzes we took. We didn't know much about the culture . . . beyond its affinity for beer and sausage. But the economy was thriving, and it was smack-dab in the middle of Europe—a great jumping-off point to other countries. And it was full of historic castles, ancient cobblestone streets . . . So far, Germany felt like the clear winner.

I yawned. We'd decide on a city later. We were heading to Asia the next day.

Southeast Asia was radically different from the narrow cobblestone roads and medieval castles of Europe, where you felt as if you were stepping back in time. Thailand was a sensory smorgasbord of spices, golden temples, and white beaches. I laughed as we wove our way across the streets of Bangkok, praying we didn't get trampled by the sea of motorbikes and tuk-tuks—colorful, motorized three-wheeled rickshaws.

At the Chatuchak Weekend Market, I indulged in coconut ice cream with mango slivers, green sticky rice, and a sprinkling of peanuts served inside a hollowed-out coconut. Each culinary experience was more sensational than the last—until I encountered black chicken, a coal-colored chicken foot perched atop vegetables. It was certainly unique.

"We'd like to go to Wat Traimit please," I told the driver of the tuk-tuk that had seen much better days.

"Okay, hop in!" he said, grinning. Everyone was always smiling in Thailand, earning it the moniker of "Land of Smiles."

We'd been hustling to as many monuments as possible, just as we had in Europe, trying to cram it all in. The Grand Palace, an ornate, delicate architectural marvel with intricate spires and glittering mosaics. Wat Po, a Buddhist temple containing a gold reclining Buddha the size of four sedans. Then we climbed a spiral staircase up to Wat Saket, also known as Golden Mountain, perched on a hill rising above the cacophony of the city.

And, on our final stop of the day was Wat Traimit, known as the Temple of the Golden Buddha—inside lay a five-and-a-half-ton, solid-gold Buddha.

"Apparently, the gold part was discovered in 1955," I summarized, reading from the plaque. "At the time, it was covered in plaster. The movers couldn't figure out why it was so heavy. When they tried to take it to its new location, the ropes broke and the statue fell to the ground, cracking the plaster and revealing its solid-gold surface."

I hadn't been able to put it into words until now, but that's what I expected it to feel like when we'd finally found the place to move abroad. I'd crack open the plaster and the golden city would be revealed. But for now, our trip to Asia let us pause the search and truly enjoy ourselves.

The day after our enchanting temple tour, we hopped on a plane from Bangkok to Krabi, then embarked on a wooden boat to Railay Bay. The long-tail boats, with their extended prows and roaring outboard engines, were like something out of *Jurassic Park*. As we sailed toward Railay Bay, the dramatic limestone cliffs came into view, and I half-expected a T. rex to emerge from the lush jungle at any moment. Neon-colored fish glided gracefully beneath our boat, adding to the surreal atmosphere.

Outside our cabana, the staff greeted us with guava drinks and spa appointments. Our suite was adorned with a grand canopy bed draped in fluttering white silk.

"I feel like this is too fancy for me," I admitted to Michael, plopping my backpack on the low wooden bench by the window.

"Can you believe this is one of the cheaper hotels? I feel like we're at the Ritz!" Michael said, turning on the showerhead. "This bathroom is the size of my dorm at A&M."

I got to enjoy our room for about five minutes. We were all set to go to dinner when a wave of fatigue hit me.

"You go ahead," I said, shooing Michael away. And climbed into the grand bed.

A minute later I projectile vomited all over that pristine white bed. I couldn't even stop midvomit to call Michael. When he finally came back, he saw the mess I'd made of our lavish room and took me straight to a clinic, where they prescribed me anti-nausea pills.

The next day, we were leaving for Cambodia. I needed to get over this thing, and fast. But as soon as we got on another long-tail boat, I hurled whatever was left in my stomach out into the sea. Those brightly colored fish now seemed to mock me, frowning up at me in disgust.

At the airport, I made a beeline for the bathroom as boarding for our flight was announced over the loudspeaker. I retched for the umpteenth time, splashed water on my face, and took a few deep breaths, then boarded the plane.

Exhausted, I fell asleep as soon as we got to the hotel in Cambodia. While I slept, Michael went to the market.

When I woke up, I was convinced I had malaria. My friend's sister had had it, and the symptoms were too similar: shaking, chills, headache, vomiting. *I am not going to die!* I thought. I wrote a note to Michael letting him know I was going to the hospital. I fell asleep again, in the middle of writing it.

I woke up when Michael came back. My shivering had stopped, and I felt like I could actually eat something. It was a miracle! Or maybe it was just food poisoning.

"Michael," I said, lifting my chin, "I almost died."

"I think you had food poisoning," he said, eyeing me carefully.

"It felt like I almost died"—I folded my arms—"so now it's time to live."

After that, the rest of the trip took on a new meaning.

I didn't want to just take photos and jot down notes for my blog. I wanted to experience everything. Okay, so food poisoning wasn't a near-death experience, but being so sick and missing out for even just a few days made me realize how special it was to be here.

Buoyed by my recovery, I felt more than ready for the next adventure: a guided tour at sunrise of Angkor Wat, the Seventh Wonder of the World. As the first rays of daylight breached the horizon in Siem Reap, the ancient temple emerged from the shroud of night in an ethereal glow. Angkor Wat's towering spires stretched up like skyscrapers, and a tranquil moat mirrored the sacred temple's reflection. And though we were surrounded by hundreds of other visitors, a stillness pervaded.

From our view, the towering spires of the temples stretched out like skyscrapers and the intricate carvings seemed to come alive. "Wait," I whispered to Michael, pointing. "Is something moving?"

Yes! As we crept closer, we saw a troop of monkeys dangling all over the massive complex of temples, dancing around the intricate carvings on every surface. It was a sight to behold.

After Cambodia, we ventured to Vietnam, taking a junk boat cruise on Ha Long Bay. The boat had only about ten cabins, each small and tidy with a porthole to view the thousands of islands dotting the emerald-green water. Along the way we explored the stalactites of Thien Canh Son cave and kayaked to hidden coves.

And finally, for our last leg of the trip, we headed to Chiang Mai for the annual Yi Peng Lantern Festival. Out of all the incredible things we'd planned in Southeast Asia, I was most excited for the festival and its thousands of paper lanterns released into the full-moon sky.

Monks clad in bright orange robes with shaved heads proceeded in, holding candles. I wiped the sweat off my face, watching them silently.

We were each handed a khom loi, a folded thin white paper lantern, and instructed to release it at nine o'clock that evening. We sat with thousands of others spread out on the open lawn, waiting for the right moment.

Per tradition, we had placed a message inside the lantern, one that would carry our prayers and well-wishes for the future.

I chose mine quite literally, writing "To find my path and pick the right place to live abroad."

Together, Michael and I released our khom loi into the sky with thousands of others. As the lanterns' warm glow reached out to touch the velvet night, the world looked as if it were dripping with stars.

I watched Michael's face under the soft glow, then grasped his hand. The paper lanterns danced in the gentle breeze, each one carrying a unique, whispered wish.

I leaned against Michael. "What did you wish for?"

"I think we wished for the same thing," he said, squeezing my hand.

The city's ancient temples stood like stencils, bathed in the lanterns' ethereal light. I listened to the murmur of enchanting incantations and the gentle strum of instruments filling the air.

I was ready to move abroad.

Picking the Present

My birthday is my most and least favorite day of the year. It's my favorite because I love attention and words of affirmation. Okay, and presents. But it's my least favorite for two reasons: first, it reminds me that I'm getting older; and second, I always put so much pressure on the day, and this often leads to disappointment.

It must be memorable! If not, I feel like I failed—that I won't have a moment to reflect upon in the future and recall how incredible it had felt. I want to collect good memories to look back on.

I wholly identify with Clark Griswold in *National Lampoon's Christmas Vacation*. All Clark wants is for the entire family to celebrate Christmas at his house with the most extravagant lights, Christmas tree, and dinner spread the world has ever known. What's the big deal?

As they are discussing Clark's plans, his wife, Ellen, reminds him, "It's just that I know how you build things up in your mind, Sparky. You set standards that no family event can ever live up to."

When things go wrong, as of course they do in the movie, Clark freaks out. I can relate.

I will always remember my perfect twelfth birthday. I had a party during the day with everyone in my grade, then my best friends came over for a slumber party. We dressed in pajamas and went to the grocery store, using carrots as cigars, then on to Blockbuster, and finished by watching *A League of Their Own* until we fell asleep. I felt so seen and so connected to my friends that day, I'd always try to re-create the feeling.

In my quest to relive my rose-colored past, I set myself up for disappointment again and again with my unrealistic expectations for the perfect birthday. Now, though, when I really look back, I know that it was the mishaps that became some of the most memorable.

But this upcoming birthday was going to be special regardless: it was the day we'd decide where to live abroad.

I knew I was in an extraordinarily privileged position. Getting to choose where to move abroad, to nearly anywhere in the world! Sure, it was scary to move my entire life: I had to secure a visa, uproot my dogs, sell my stuff, make new friends, change phone numbers—everything required to create a new life. It was a risk but a calculated one. And I had a backup plan. If all else failed, we could go home and move back into our house in Dallas or even in with my parents. Taking that leap of faith is much less daunting when you have a safety net waiting to catch you if you fall.

The final tether to our life at home—what kept us from taking the plunge—seemed to have fallen away: both my dad's and Michael's mom's cancers were in remission. My dad had taken on a medical trial for his stage 3C melanoma and prostate cancer, which had proved successful. Michael's mom's rare inflammatory breast cancer was finally responding to the treatments.

Back home from Asia, we really, really needed to decide where to live. Making this choice would seal our fate and propel us to actually make the move.

Germany was the country. At this point, Michael and I both thrived on the novelty of getting out of our comfort zone, and picking a place we'd never even stepped foot in before felt terrifyingly exhilarating. Germany had all the criteria for a place we'd want to live, so now we just had to pick a city.

The problem for me was trying to pick the perfect place. A place that would have everything I ever wanted. A place that would instantly feel familiar but also exciting enough to feel foreign.

"I don't know, Michael," I said, throwing a rock at Percy Priest Lake near our house. "I feel like Antwerp was pretty ideal."

"That's just your nostalgia talking." Michael casually tossed a rock and I watched as it skidded across the water, making three perfect hops before plopping into the lake. "You remember that first trip to Europe and glorify it."

I nodded. I couldn't argue.

"Remember in Belgium when we tried to grab a 'quick' bite to eat?" he continued.

"Yes, I do," I said, laughing. "Those elusive European waiters. I know, I know. It's not perfect."

I tend to romanticize things. Especially the past. Whenever I feel itchy, unhappy, worried, or stressed in the present, I reflect. Nostalgia can trap me, allowing me to avoid making tough decisions. When I escape into a happy time in the past, I glaze over any flaws and cast it all in a positive light. But I've come to realize that I need to consider what hasn't worked and what I want to change about my life. No place could be perfect, and I was ready to loosen my grip on the past and to still remember it and use it but embrace the future.

As we walked around the lake, I watched Millie fling herself headlong into the water as Hugo dipped his toes in. Yes! I thought. I needed to be more like Millie. I needed to take the plunge.

So we decided: we would pick a place to live by my birthday.

Cologne, Stuttgart, Hamburg, Dusseldorf, and Munich were at the top of our list. But none of them felt quite right.

So we spent the rest of the day researching other options. I was feeling a little burned-out on scrolling online, but I typed in "Germany expat city," and this time a city I hadn't heard of popped up: Heidelberg.

I clicked onto a travel blog. When I swept over the image of a fairy-tale castle atop a hill gazing down on a bridge, a river, and a storybook village, I felt a ripple of intrigue. I'd never even heard of this city. Hands trembling with excitement, I typed in "pictures of Heidelberg, Germany."

I added it to our list of places we were considering and jotted down some notes.

Pros: Beautiful, Castle

Cons:

Well, cons, I left blank for now.

It was centrally located in Europe. Not too big, not too small.

From that glimpse online, I saw a moving picture of what my life could look like in the very near future rolling out before me as if on an old projector.

I ran in to show Michael, holding out my laptop with the fairy-tale picture of the castle and the river pixelated on the screen.

His eyes widened.

He glanced up at me. "Hmm, that does seem beautiful."

Michael dutifully added Heidelberg to the spreadsheet. In the notes column, he wrote: idyllic looking. I added an asterisk next to Heidelberg on my own spreadsheet. Michael and I kept our notes separate as not to sway the final decision.

"Let's do some independent research, and by Sunday we'll get together and choose the city," Michael said formally, as if we'd be orchestrating a company merger.

Something about Heidelberg felt right to me. But I kept looking online, searching for a place that checked all the boxes. As I closed my laptop, an image of Michael and me walking along the Neckar River with the dogs popped into my mind. It wouldn't be perfect—nothing would be—but it seemed right.

Afraid to feel disappointed if Michael chose somewhere else, I decided to curb my expectations. No place is perfect, I kept repeating to myself. Maybe Michael had a different idea. Whatever it was, we would make it work.

On Sunday, I put on a black dress and curled my hair. For this momentous occasion, I wanted to look the part. I sauntered into Michael's office, carefully placing my laptop on the bed. I called the dogs into the room and shut the door. They deserved some insight into the decision-making process.

"You ready?" I asked.

"Let's just say it on the count of three," he replied.

In unison, we counted: "One, two, three . . . HEIDELBERG!"

I leapt up and flung my arms around Michael's neck.

"It felt right, but I . . . had . . . to . . . check," he said, his voice a little choked from my hug crushing his airway. I let go. "It's the perfect place," he continued. "It's close to Frankfurt airport. It's a university town—actually, it has the oldest university in Germany!"

I only squealed, so he went on.

"It wasn't bombed in the war and looks picturesque. A lot of the buildings are from the sixteenth century."

"We are moving to Heidelberg!" I shrieked.

In my joy, I'd completely forgotten to have a backward glance at the past. I didn't even panic over the fact that I was another year older or whether or not it was the perfect day. I was too excited for our future.

No More Countdowns

"My cancer is back."

It wasn't my dad calling this time—it was Michael's mom. A few years ago she'd beaten a rare form of breast cancer. But now it was back.

In my head, the disease was scary but treatable. After a few glimpses of cancer with close family and friends, I knew it was dreadful. But it wasn't insurmountable. Especially breast cancer.

Right?

"Well, the good news is that we'll be home soon and can help around the house," I said.

Our plan was to move back to Dallas for a month before moving abroad to Heidelberg.

"It's different this time," she spoke quietly, solemnly. She was defeated. "I guess I don't need my countdown to retirement after all."

Michael and I packed up all of our belongings, now far fewer after a garage sale, and left Nashville for the ten-hour drive to Dallas. When we arrived, we knew things weren't going well.

Jan was dying. The cancer had spread to her brain and was progressing rapidly. She had weeks, months, at best.

Michael immediately stepped into action. Some people crumble in difficult situations. Michael plans and forges ahead. I watched as he carefully organized the dog's medical records, his Texas A&M Aggie ring, and his keys on my old dresser with detailed precision. We were staying at my parents' house before the move, in my old bedroom. The plan was to be there a week. Now we didn't know how long we'd stay.

Michael, along with his aunt and uncle, took charge of what needed to be done. They found hospice care where she could be comfortable.

Together, we got Jan settled into her new, final home. Everything was beige. The walls, the bedding, the carpets, the bathroom sink. Even the lighting cast a beige glow. Maybe the absence of bright colors was supposed to point to calm, to cleanliness, but it just made me feel sad—it felt sterile and unfamiliar.

So we tried to bring in items that would make her feel more at home: pictures of her grandkids, a blue pillow from her bedroom, a hand-sewn quilt from the couch, a picture of Ivan. The Russian blue had died only a few months before, as if he knew Jan wouldn't be far behind.

"I want you to go," Jan said, weakly holding Michael's hand as she sat propped up in her beige bed.

"Mom, don't worry about that right now," he responded.

"No, Michael, you need to go."

She could barely speak, but she wanted this to be known.

I leaned on the guest bench and pressed my back to the wall, trying to let mother and son have this moment.

Michael's grandmother, Jan's mother, entered the room, putting on a brave smile. She sat next to Jan's bed and watched her daughter slip further and further away. Every day, we went to the hospice center and watched Michael's mother slowly deteriorate, growing thinner and more frail. She wasn't eating or speaking anymore.

Grandmother, as we called her, was cautiously hesitant about our move abroad. Her parents had immigrated to the United States from Czechia (then Czechoslovakia) for a better life. She couldn't quite wrap her head around why we would want to leave the United States, a place that had so much opportunity.

Many relatives voiced the same concern.

"Don't you like living here?" they'd ask.

"It's not that I don't like it here," I'd answer. "It's that I want to experience something different—to learn about other places. To travel more."

They would nod, still unsure why we would leave the freedom of our country behind.

As the sun was just beginning to come up, Michael and I sat side by side at my parents' kitchen table, our laptops open. The sun flitted through the blinds and cast a warm glow around him. He sat upright, scanned his screen, trying to sift through the fine print of our airline tickets.

"Oh, look." He pointed. "We can just change the dates."

I was in awe of his calm demeanor. Every day, he continued to show up for his mom and for me, taking charge of our travel logistics and seeking out hours when I could work on my blog.

"Let's just push it back a month, August fifteenth to September fifteenth. It says we can change it again if needed."

When I awoke on the morning of August 15, a peculiar mixture of emotions stirred within me: Happiness. Fear. Longing. Today we were supposed to be leaving for our great adventure abroad, but fate had had other plans. Sometimes life's priorities shift in ways we can't control or predict. I felt grateful that we were still here, able to provide support and comfort to Jan and the family.

The hospice center seemed extra quiet that day. Michael and I walked in, as we had every day, me carrying my laptop under my arm as we held hands. Michael's grandmother, aunt, and uncle were already there, forming a semicircle around Jan's bed. But today was different.

"It looks like this might be her last day on earth," Michael's uncle said, stoically uncrossing his legs and standing up.

Michael pulled up a chair next to his mother's bed and whispered to her, "You don't have to be in pain. You can go now."

And that was it. She took a final breath as we held ours. A thick wave of sadness rippled through the beige room.

She was gone, and how remarkable that her last day on earth was the day we'd chosen to move abroad. I took it as a sign, as a nod to our move. She was letting go, and we could leave now without strings of guilt holding us back.

In the days that followed, Michael organized the funeral, navigating the details for the casket, the flowers, and the donations Jan had requested for the Susan G. Komen Breast Cancer Foundation, all through a haze of grief.

I wrote Jan's obituary. It was a big task, to reflect on someone's life. It made me wonder, If I were to die today, what would my obituary say about me?

I've always thought about my legacy, but there's nothing quite like the passing of someone close to you to confront the reality of your own impermanence; mortality has a way of putting things into perspective. It's easy to get caught up in the everyday minutiae of life, but now, faced with the reality of death, I found it impossible not to pause and think about what truly mattered. What kind of impact did I want to leave on the world? What memories would people carry of me when I'm gone? And really . . . who the hell was I?

The days seemed to pass by in a flash, and Michael continued to hold his head high, not willing to wallow for even a second.

As we stood together at the funeral, united in our sorrow, I felt a renewed sense of conviction. Through Jan's passing, I had seen firsthand how fragile life was, and how important it was to pursue our dreams. This move abroad, our great adventure . . . it had become more than just a personal journey; it was a testament to Jan's memory, a reminder to live life fully, to embrace every opportunity that came our way.

Michael cried silently during the eulogy. I had been crying all day. Tears had already flowed mercilessly for me, and now it was time for me to hold it together for him. I dried my eyes and held his hand tightly, squeezing it to let him know it was okay to let go.

When I picture Jan now, I don't see the tubes in her mouth, the hospital bed, the beige room.

Her cheeks are rosy. Her hair is long. And she's asking me, "What exactly are you planning to do with my son?" It was a memory that had once made me angry with her—she'd caught me and Michael all those years ago as teenagers, when she'd come home early from choir practice. I wasn't supposed to be there.

But that's the beautiful thing about memories: they are malleable with time. We can make new meaning of them. Now, that memory of her worried about who exactly Michael had gotten himself caught up with makes me smile. Because it reminds me of the woman that she was, one who cared deeply and fiercely. One who wanted the best for her son. And one, I think, who would approve of the path we were embarking on.

The next few weeks shuffled by in a haze. But anticipation in light of our grief often felt wrong—how could we muster up excitement to move abroad after everything that had happened? We found it hard to . . . but we also found it hard not to. Moving day was quickly approaching.

I looked at the countdown on my phone, ticking down the days until our move abroad. I deleted it.

No more countdowns in life. It was time to start living.

Talks to the Moon

When I was young, my father and I attended Adventure Guides, a program put on by the YMCA as a chance for children and their fathers to experience nature away from city living and build companionship through outdoor adventure activities.

Dads and daughters would load up minivans with brand-new hiking boots, tents, hot dogs, marshmallows, and walking sticks, and head to Camp Classen, an idyllic plot of 2,200 acres in the Arbuckle Mountains of southern Oklahoma. After that two-hour drive, I felt as if I'd been transported to a different world. My dad; my best friend, Hayley; Hayley's dad, Ed; and I were always the first to arrive and the last to leave. Eventually the staff gave our dads the keys to lock the gate.

Throughout the weekend, we'd ride horses, splash in the lake, and tell ghost stories. But first, I would climb into a wheelbarrow meant to transport luggage, and my dad would push me down the hill in front of our cabin at breakneck speed over uneven ground. It was risky fun, and the only other dad-daughter duo brave enough to join in was Hayley and Ed. My mom would have been apoplectic if she'd seen these wild rides. Despite being a sometimes nervous child, I loved it—the controlled chaos of it all. It was my version of living on the edge. It was pushing boundaries.

My mom was ever-present on those campouts too, despite not being there. She'd help come up with all the skits and our camp names. Dad's was Mad Dog because sometimes after hanging up the phone in the newsroom, he'd bark. And sometimes he'd bark even before hanging up.

Mom came up with my nickname: Talks to the Moon. She'd often pull me outside whenever the moon was big and bright, no matter how old I got. She would point up to the moon and say, "Far away as you may be, the same moon that shines on you also shines on me." And so on those weekends away I did talk to the moon, knowing that I could always look to it perched high in the sky and feel my mom whenever I missed her.

At the end of those weekends, we'd perform skits around a bonfire, and then the leader of the guides, my future best friend's dad, Tom Shortall, would hand out painted rocks to those who'd shown bravery. My dad got a painted rock at every single campout because he always won the chubby-bunny contest, a competition to determine who could stuff the most marshmallows in their mouth. My dad was a Pulitzer Prize–winning journalist who had met President Clinton, but I was more impressed by his skill at cramming several globs of sugar in his mouth. That, and the fact that our skits were unequivocally the best.

Our most infamous skit was called "Important Papers." A king (my dad, wearing a makeshift crown, sat on a throne—which, in this case, was a folding camping chair we'd draped with a sheet) looked out at the audience and bellowed, "Where are my important papers?"

In turn, each girl in my crew would rush up and hand him what they thought he wanted: a rolled-up newspaper, official-looking documents, a notebook. He'd cast each aside, yelling, "Those are not my important papers!"

Finally I'd march out, beaming, carrying a stick with a roll of toilet paper on top. The king would grasp the stick, yank off the toilet roll, and dramatically pull the paper to his chest, caressing it.

"Ahh, these are my important papers!"

The audience would go wild, and we'd bow.

Now this is living, I thought.

The night before we left for Germany, my mom pulled me outside, and together we looked up at the moon. I watched her face, bathed in ethereal moonlight.

"You know," I said, "you inspire me."

"I do?" she said, turning to me. "That means a lot."

"I feel like you're more than just my mom—you're my spiritual guardian, leading me to the path of righteousness and world domination."

"That's good, Helene. Write that down. Maybe one day you'll use it in a book." She smiled.

"I'm really scared," I breathed.

"You should be. It would be weird if you weren't."

I nodded, silent.

"The problem is you look up and onward. You're driven," she told me. "I'm proud of that. But sometimes it's hard because it means I have to let you go."

We stood there, tears welling in my eyes as we looked up at the moon. Nostalgia always creeps up on me; I want to look back. I want to focus on the good old days. But in that moment, my guilt was crushing me. Here I was, standing with my mom who was very much alive. And I was leaving. I was leaving everything I knew behind to enter a country I had never even stepped foot in before. The girl who never wanted to leave home, the girl who despised change and relished the memories from her past.

Was I making a mistake?

"Won't it be hard to leave friends and family behind?" many of my friends had asked me.

Of course, you idiots! I'd wanted to say. But instead I answered, "They're going to come and visit me." Still, I ached at the thought of not being on the same continent as my parents. My heroes.

And the reality was, I would be missing out. When we left, three of my friends were pregnant with their first babies. Other friends were pregnant with their second children. A friend asked me to be in her wedding, and I had to decline. The wedding was in October, just one month after we would have moved abroad. Our plan was to visit home only once in the two or three years we lived in Germany. I couldn't just move and then come right back.

"The food in Germany is terrible," a former coworker warned. I couldn't argue, as I had no idea—I'd never been to Germany. But I let their comments slide off my back, impervious to their impressions. I'd make up my own mind when we arrived.

"I could never do that," others trilled. It wasn't a compliment. It was an admission that there was something just not right.

Or maybe they thought we were giving up. Balking at responsibilities.

"So, you're just jet-setting off to Europe, huh?" a relative asked at Thanksgiving. "Must be nice, no responsibilities."

I felt the weight of our visa paperwork, my budding blog business, our dogs' medical records and vaccinations, a full year of research, and several years of dreams pressing down on us. All these documents were my important papers.

As humans, often when we don't understand something, we dismiss it or even invalidate it, trying to put it in its place. Different is often synonymous with wrong. *What's wrong with them?* I imagined my criticizers said in bed at night, pulling the covers up as they settled into the security that they were right.

Michael and I had gone to good schools, we had good parents, we had college degrees. Michael even had his master's. We'd bought a house and owned two dogs. Why would we throw away all that stability to "jet-set" off to Europe? But we didn't look at it that way. To us, we were taking a measured risk.

No, I wouldn't be visiting home anytime soon. First I needed to prove the naysayers wrong.

And I knew I was making that same girl who talked to the moon proud.

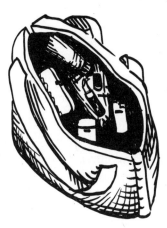

But What about My Lipsticks?

My alarm buzzed unnecessarily. I'd been up every hour throughout the night, checking the clock to make sure I hadn't missed the wakeup call. Our flight wasn't until three that afternoon, but there were still so many things I needed to do.

Like get my two suitcases under the weight limit of fifty pounds to fly from Dallas, Texas, to Frankfurt, Germany.

I scrutinized the two open suitcases, an army inspector checking a soldier's uniform, looking for anything out of place or extraneous.

Michael had found four used suitcases on Craigslist, and we had stuffed them with everything we thought we'd need for when we lived in Germany—which, apparently for me, was a lot of lipstick.

I looked up at the picture frames in my childhood bedroom: a photo of me and my dad from an Adventure Guides camping trip; a family photo from my wedding day; one of Michael and me from our senior year of high school, next to the glass slipper my grandmother had given me when I played Cinderella in the seventh grade.

Should I pack those too?

No.

But what about the lipsticks?

Some people collect stamps or Beanie Babies. But I—as I realized for the first time—collected lipsticks. I don't think I'd ever thrown one away. From the Maybelline Baby Lips I'd bought in eighth grade and worn to my middle-school dances to the rosy-mauve twenty-four-hour Revlon lipstick I'd worn on my wedding day, I'd managed to save all of them. Each one a token of my past and therefore a piece of my identity. Recently MAC Cosmetics had even sent me twenty-five of their new liquid lipsticks for free. I was on their PR list. Me! This meant that they'd occasionally send me free makeup. I felt that, despite not getting paid, having a major brand know that I existed meant I was on the right track with my blog. Those lipsticks were crossing the Atlantic with me, fifty-pound weight limit be damned.

Because what part of my personality would I relinquish if I tossed these lipsticks? I'd never thought of myself as someone who got emotionally attached to material objects—until I had to get rid of some. Tasked with choosing only a select few lipsticks made me realize just how much I identified with them.

I had already carefully put away our nostalgic items in boxes and stored them on a metal shelf in my parents' converted garage. Inside were things I deemed too important to throw away. The homecoming chrysanthemum Michael had given me for our first date our senior year of high school. In Texas, dates exchange large "mums"—huge fake flowers, nearly the size of a melon, made out of ribbon—to wear to homecoming games the night before the dance. The long ribbons usually hold a bit of flair like glittery stickers of the year and your date's name, as well as quarter-sized plastic footballs. Oh, the memories. I just couldn't let it go.

I also couldn't let go of my signed Britney Spears poster, every note a friend or family member had ever written to me, and photo albums that were now absolutely digitized and backed up online and on my computer.

Okay, fine. So I guess I did have an emotional connection to some things.

I struggled with how many pairs of socks to bring. Do I move with enough socks for a week? A month? Years? I somehow didn't factor in that we would have a washer and dryer in our new home and that obviously Germany would have stores that sold socks. And lipstick, for that matter. I kept forgetting that this was a move—a relocation and not a vacation.

Michael, despite being an accidental minimalist, was struggling too. He would be carrying all the dogs' stuff in addition to his own things. He'd neatly packed his dry-fit shirts, five long-sleeve and seven short-sleeve moisture-wicking shirts, along with seven pairs of shorts and four pairs of moisture-wicking cargo pants that he'd researched for weeks before purchasing.

"It's my Europe wardrobe," he said proudly, modeling his new clothes for me in the bedroom we'd soon be leaving behind. Michael had never cared about clothing, which is something I've always admired about him. Dallas is an image- and fashion-conscious city, and seemingly everyone we grew up with wore name brands. Michael, on the other hand, wore things until they fell apart.

Next he carefully folded up his jeans and coat from middle school and placed them in his suitcase.

When he'd first put on that coat one cold day after we'd graduated from college, I'd pointed out a hole in his left forearm sleeve.

"Oh yeah, thanks," he'd said, inspecting it. Then he marched over to the kitchen drawer, ripped off a piece of duct tape, and stuck it to the hole. He glanced over at me, giving a thumbs-up. And I fell deeper in love.

But even with Michael's minimalism, our bags were still slightly over the weight limit. A few things would need to go.

My mom's love language is gift giving. I've never left the house without her giving me something—whether it was a Peter Rabbit plate that I used as a child or a new shirt she thought I would like.

So, when she handed Michael and me each a package, I wasn't at all surprised. It was a bunch of things we might need during the journey to Germany: wet wipes, travel-sized toothpaste, toothbrushes, dog treats (that were probably expired), protein bars, soft peppermints (would also need to check the expiration date on those), and a note for each of us. But Michael got one extra thing: beard oil.

With our bags packed like Tetris cubes, stuffed with everything we thought we'd need, it was time to head to the airport.

Mom made us a sign that read, Gone to Germany #HellYeahHeidelberg. I'd come up with that hashtag, one that I planned to use across social media posts for our life abroad.

We posed in front of my childhood home with our four suitcases, two dogs, and our sign, like kids ready for their first day of school. We were brimming with nerves and excitement.

As we made the forty-five-minute drive to the DFW airport, I gazed out the window, trying to sear into my brain how everything looked, hoping that things wouldn't change too much after I left. But that's the thing about the passage of time—with it, everything changes.

I saw birds sitting on power lines, chirping to one another, and I wondered: Why not go to the countryside or somewhere with more trees and nature? Then I realized that food is plentiful here, and it's often just tossed on the side of the road. Easy pickings. Maybe it's not as pretty here, but it's easier. And don't humans follow the same logic? We often stay in the same places because it's what we know. It's easier. It's harder to live outside of our comfort zones.

So did that mean I had changed? I still felt like the same girl who'd danced barefoot in the backyard and sung, "I'm walking right down the middle of Main Street, U.S.A." I was still the one Michael had asked to the homecoming dance.

Maybe we, as humans, don't really change—but, I thought, it's never too late to change your life. You're allowed to live differently. I still had the homecoming mum and my lipsticks. But I could start my own business and move abroad, even if the "before" me had thought I'd always live in Dallas and raise children. I knew that I was still me, but the trajectory of my life had definitely changed.

I still felt like myself, but not in my wildest dreams had I ever thought I'd own my own business, move abroad, or choose a path of such radical change. But I'd learned that I didn't have to live my life the same way I'd been living it or conform to others' expectations. My options were unlimited, confined only by my own perceptions. I had to make a choice and that choice necessitated change.

As a kid, I was extremely fearful. If someone driving a motorcycle pulled up next to our car, I would shout at my mom to drive away. The roar of the engine freaked me out.

I can also remember taking a trip with my parents to San Francisco when my dad was working on a story for the *Dallas Morning News* about low-income housing. Mom and I had spent the day watching the seals, visiting the Painted Ladies houses, and shopping. A homeless man followed me into a Walgreens, and I was done. I wanted to go home. Immediately. A once-a-year trip to the beach was enough for me.

But I'd since outgrown those fears. Now my biggest fear was regret.

"Do you have any regrets?" I asked my dad a few nights before the move.

"Regrets," he said thoughtfully, "are for people who've never tried. Maybe I haven't succeeded at everything I've done, but at least I've tried. Most people's biggest impediment is their self-censorship. They don't try because they worry they might fail. Life is a self-fulfilling prophecy."

I wrote that down. I knew I'd need it later.

I took out a few lipsticks and handed them to my mom.

"Here," I said. "I think these colors would look great on you."

"Thanks!" she said, beaming. "A little memento before you leave. I'll think of you when I wear them."

To the outside world, we looked like chaotic decision-makers. Irrational, even. We had both quit our jobs, my new "little blog business" was only in its infancy, and here we were leaving the country with only what we could carry. Moving to a country we'd never stepped foot in before. I was desperate to prove the proverbial "everyone" wrong. But mostly I wanted to prove to myself that we could do it.

This homebody was leaving home.

We're Not in Texas Anymore

For the twelve-hour flight from Dallas to Frankfurt, I'd had plenty of time to overthink our decision to leave every comfort we'd known behind to move to Germany. We'd packed up our lives—leaving behind (or selling) most of our belongings—to move to a country we'd never even seen before. Were we making the right choice?

I'm always jealous of people who can read on flights. Michael often churns through a Cormac McCarthy novel even as the plane thrusts up and down with turbulence. Meanwhile, I search for relief by directing the air vent directly at my face and pulling my hair off my neck into a ponytail, sometimes chanting to myself, "Do not throw up, do not throw up." I get incredible motion sickness, and it's all I can do to just focus on breathing. And for this flight, I couldn't even sleep. I was left alone with my thoughts.

Truthfully, I get some of my best pondering done during long flights. I often save up my introspection for when I'm in a tin can thirty thousand feet above the earth.

I started rummaging through the filing cabinets of my mind for potential disasters, but we'd already taken care of all the responsibilities we could think of. We'd rented out our house, which covered our monthly mortgage payment. We'd also managed to save up $45,000 for emergencies abroad: if we got hurt or made some bad financial decisions, we had a cushion. We purchased health insurance from Care Concept to cover us overseas, which only cost $164.53 per month for the pair of us. The dogs had all their shots, records, microchips, and veterinary health certificates. We were required to have a USDA-accredited vet do a checkup and sign and complete a form before we left and with a simple signature, now our dogs were ready to be citizens of Germany. It wasn't as easy for us, the humans. We still needed a visa to live in Germany legally.

We had booked a hotel for a week so we could hit the ground running to get our visas and find a place to live. But I still felt absolutely unnerved. On paper, the trajectory of our life together had always been the white picket fence. The big house, kids, dogs, and dependable jobs. And it wasn't that we shunned that lifestyle. But not everyone wants the same thing, and not everyone even knows what they want until they ask that question of themselves and search for the answer. We were on a quest to find out what we wanted and, in doing so, departed from the world we had known. It was jarring but also exciting.

As the plane descended, the clouds parted, giving way to clusters of red-tiled roofs and tiny plots of green, then buildings and church steeples. Lush hillsides were speckled with more houses and gardens. Is that a castle? I wondered. Even from the plane, I could tell we weren't in Dallas, or even the US, anymore. "Millie," I said serenely, leaning over to pet our spaniel, "we aren't in Kansas anymore." Like Dorothy in *The Wizard of Oz*, we were stepping into unfamiliar, magical territory. I gave my seat belt an extra tug as if to secure me for what was to come. We had chosen to let go of the so-called guarantees of our future, boldly stepping into the unknown, heading down our own yellow-brick road.

When we arrived in Frankfurt, we took the dogs out to pee. "This is it," we told them, though we were really telling ourselves: This is our new home.

From Frankfurt we hopped on a forty-five-minute shuttle ride into Heidelberg, the dogs sleeping lazily by our feet. I wished I could be as calm as they were, but my heart raced.

As we rounded the corner, literally our entire lives at our feet, I felt a moment of panic. I grasped at my purse, checking to make sure I had our passports and paperwork. But they were all there, my important papers neatly smiling up at me.

Balancing a dog leash in one hand and the handles of my two rolling suitcases in the other, we went up to the check-in desk at the B&B Hotel Heidelberg. I was eager to use some of the German I'd studied. "Hallo!"

"Checking in?" answered a woman with a golden tan, bleached-blond hair, and deep-set frown lines, not looking up from the computer.

"Yes, thank you." Michael and I exchanged grins and raised eyebrows in acknowledgment that she spoke English. An immediate relief.

"You're on floor five," she said, handing over the keys but barely glancing at us.

I wanted to shout out, "We just moved here from another continent!" or "This is our first time stepping foot in Germany, guten tag!" But I didn't. I took the keys and headed toward the elevator, passing vending machines full of packaged goods like Chipsfrisch Paprika, Kinder Bueno, and Hit Coco Creme.

We couldn't all fit in the tiny elevator with our luggage, so I took Hugo and Millie up first, then Michael came up second with the bags. We dropped our suitcases, which swallowed up nearly all the available space in our room. Two single beds had been pushed together to form one, and two nightstands were attached to the walls on each side. A small bathroom neatly fit a shower, miniature sink, and toilet. Open shelving held an iron, extra sheets, and pillows. Immediately, Hugo stood with his front legs perched on the windowsill. He gazed out, surveying his new home country, a king looking down on his kingdom. After all, as a Doberman, this was the country of his ancestors.

"Let's go, the light should be perfect right now." Michael reviewed the map. "We can head to the Old Town—the Altstadt—and check out the main street."

We walked to the closest tram stop, six minutes on foot from the hotel. Thankfully, the tram system was straightforward and easy to navigate.

One of the reasons we'd chosen Heidelberg was the fact that it had been left unscathed in World War II; the town had essentially remained unchanged since the last fire—in 1693. The river ran parallel to the street, a red sandstone bridge spanning it. The bridge held intricately carved statues, reminiscent of Charles Bridge in Prague, and at its end was the entrance—two white towers—to the Old Town. Across the river, the hills rose up, stacked with mansions and apartments.

As I stepped off the platform onto the cobblestone streets of Heidelberg, I knew we'd made the right decision in moving here. Walking the long street as it snaked its way toward the castle, we glanced in awe at the sandstone buildings, intricate archways, and buzzing shoppers. We were discovering an entirely new universe.

Shops, cafés, and church steeples peeked out like bunny ears along the Hauptstrasse. Shoppers buzzed through the streets with their market bags and coffees, talking rapidly in German. We stood there, immobilized, trying to soak it all in.

The castle perched above it all, quiet and imposing, echoing of queens and kings from centuries past. Oddly, it made me think of Doctor T. J. Eckleburg, the pair of bespectacled eyes on the billboard from *The Great Gatsby*, only he was gazing approvingly down at the city.

As day drifted into night, the lights began to twinkle on the castle. I felt as if I were walking through a fairy tale.

"I think we should do three years instead of just two," I said without looking at Michael, still mesmerized by our new home. Even the doors to ordinary buildings were magnificent.

"Yeah, I think so too," Michael responded, squeezing my hand.

"We did it!" I said, a grin creeping onto my face.

"We live here," he confirmed, the excitement in his voice matching my own.

Beer Rules

After months of paring down our belongings, everything we owned now fit into four suitcases. But I didn't feel like I was missing out on anything. It had felt scary, painful even, to get rid of my stuff. Now I realized I didn't even need half the stuff I'd brought.

At the garage sale we'd held to try to sell most of our stuff, I nearly cried getting rid of an oversized fluffy pink sweater. It was pretty, but honestly? I didn't wear it all that much. It didn't matter, though. Much like with my lipsticks, when it had come time to part with that sweater, I was relinquishing a part of my identity, my personality. But now that we were here in Germany, the things I'd thought I couldn't live without no longer crossed my mind.

Purging all our stuff made me realize I didn't need much. After that fleeting period of nostalgia, I didn't miss my four thermoses, seven cream-colored sweaters (I really do love a good cream-colored sweater, but one or two would suffice), jewelry dishes, waffle maker, or old stickers I'd used to make a yearly scrapbook. I hadn't made a scrapbook in six years.

I'd been so caught up in consumerism, but it was truly freeing once I realized I could easily go without—I knew I had everything I needed. I was comfortable. I was happy. And it had nothing to do with things—especially the quest for new things.

In fact, I realized I'd actually brought too much with me. I certainly didn't need all those socks and plain T-shirts. I could buy them again if I needed them.

Michael has always owned few objects (five or six shirts, seven pants, five shorts), and he's one of the happiest people I know. Right before we left, Michael went searching for his new "Europe wardrobe," the clothes he'd wear to fit in with our new, more stylish Europeans since we'd be residents. I'm not sure what he thought he'd find at a thrift shop, but he hates spending money on clothes unless they'll last him a decade or more. Despite standing at six feet two, he still proudly wears his down coat from middle school (yes, the one with the duct tape) where a few holes mark the passage of time.

He'd picked up a few short-sleeve button-down shirts and jeans from the thrift shop. He had yet to wear any of them—instead, wearing his dry-fit shirts daily. And on sunny days, Michael often wore flip-flops—a fashion choice that often turned heads. For Germans, those kinds of shoes were only sensibly worn at the beach.

But now it was time to buy lederhosen to gear up for Oktoberfest. For some reason, Michael was willing to pay for high-quality leather lederhosen shorts connected by suspenders like overalls—hopefully they would last him a lifetime. I'd get a dirndl, a traditional Bavarian dress with a tight-fitting bodice at the top and a full skirt extending just past the knees.

For three weeks from the end of September to the beginning of October, Germans throw one of the biggest, grandest parties in the world dedicated to beer. For a serious people, they were also serious about partying. We couldn't wait to go.

We bought train tickets and rode three hours from Heidelberg to Munich and hit the ground running upon arrival, yanking off our travel clothes and changing into our lederhosen and dirndl in the train station bathroom before stuffing our backpacks into lockers. Then we hopped on the tram to Theresienwiese, the festival grounds. On the ride over, I stood with one arm wrapped around a pole for balance as I put my hair in two braids.

"'The Oktoberfest tradition in Munich began in 1810 as a celebration of the royal wedding between Crown Prince Ludwig and Princess Therese of Saxe-Hildburghausen,'" Michael read from his phone, straight from Britannica, preparing us as if someone would be testing us on Oktoberfest history.

"'Theresienwiese, or Therese's Meadow, is in honor of the princess, and they hosted a grand horse race on October 17, 1810, which marked the culmination of the wedding celebration. The event was such a success that it was decided to hold a similar celebration the following year, giving birth to the annual Oktoberfest tradition.'" Michael paused, then looked around, beaming. "This is perfect. This is the exact introduction to Germany we need." He pulled on the leather straps of his lederhosen, looking like a country boy on his way to the circus for the first time.

It was a crisp, cool day in September, as if even God knew it was Oktoberfest. Before moving to Heidelberg, I'd heard more about Oktoberfest than anything else when it came to German culture. I imagined it to be a boozy bacchanal filled with drunk, sloppy men tossing beer into the air, like our Oktoberfest celebrations in Dallas. In fact, watching a YouTube video about Tomorrowland during Dallas's Oktoberfest in 2011 had led me to moving abroad in the first place.

But of course Oktoberfest in Munich was worlds different from Oktoberfest in Dallas. As I stepped through the gates, I was immediately enveloped in the atmosphere. Huge tents festooned with wreaths, flowers, wooden balconies, and insignia of beer brands gave the effect of a beer-themed amusement park. Instead of roller coasters and carnival games, we were met with overflowing beer steins and laughter; instead of cheap chicken fingers, we saw mouthwatering pretzels, a whole rotisserie ox roasting, and sausages. In addition to the tents, there were a few rides, games, and restaurants.

We went on a Tuesday to avoid crowds; apparently, this was the right idea. We immediately got a table at Löwenbräu, a popular tent, and sat with other festivalgoers at one big table. The sound of clinking glass, inside our warmly lit tent, the smell of roasted nuts wafting through the air, and the sight of brightly colored dirndls and chocolate-brown leather lederhosen made for a spectacular scene. Colorful banners of blue and white hung from the ceiling and walls, and ribbons dangled from the chandeliers. Row upon row of wooden benches and tables were packed to the brim with red-cheeked men and women. A wooden platform for the musicians sat in the center of it all, adorned with flags and hand-carved wooden steins.

"Where are you from?" a man in a salmon-colored button-down and lederhosen asked in a German accent.

How could he tell we were American?!

"Texas! But we just moved to Heidelberg," I yelled over the cacophony.

"Welcome to the party! I am from Munich. I'm coming here just for lunch and a beer."

"Thank you! This is amazing. It's our first time here. Our first day," I answered as Michael ordered beer.

"Oh, then I will teach you," Salmon Shirt Guy said. "When you cheers—*prost*—you must look into everyone's eyes, or you have bad sex or luck for seven years. I say bad sex, much worse." He looked me squarely in the eye as he spoke, as if to convey the gravity of the superstition. When the beer maid came back, carrying nearly a dozen liter-sized steins to the table with Herculean strength, we all clinked glasses, deliberately pausing to look each person in the eye.

"Look." The man pointed to another man halfway around the room. "He is standing on the table, so he must chug his beer entirely." It was only around one in the afternoon, so most people were seated. He told us that later everyone would be standing on benches to watch the live music. He also mentioned that if we happened to see someone passed out, they were most likely not German.

"Let's try to get to every single tent, Helene," Michael said. He has a sixth sense about crowds, and as the day wore on into the night, the crowds grew and grew. But we would go home that evening knowing we managed to venture into every tent.

Our next stop was to the cerulean blue Hacker-Festzelt, whose tent showcased a mascot that looked like a red baby drinking beer. Upon entering, we were welcomed by a celestial-themed interior: a dazzling blue sky adorned with fluffy white clouds painted on the ceiling, the heavenly backdrop inspired by the brewery's slogan, "Himmel der Bayern" (Bavarian's Heaven). The mural in the tent looked as if Leonardo da Vinci could have had a hand in it.

"So they'll just take all of this down in a couple of weeks?" I asked Michael.

He nodded. "Yep."

"I am overwhelmed in the best way possible."

We made new friends at our next table, this time a group of young women from Stuttgart.

"Our beer is the best beer," a pretty girl with almond eyes and blond hair said. "We have rules about everything—beer, too. The ingredients for beer must be water, barley malt, and hops. And that's it. Nothing else."

As we hopped from tent to tent, we learned that Germans were very forthcoming about everything we foreigners needed to know about Oktoberfest.

"Are you single?" one woman asked me.

"No, this is my husband." I hiccupped and pointed up at Michael.

"Your dirndl is wrong. There is a tradition about how you tie the ribbon on your dirndl. Right is for taken, left is for single, center is for virgin, and back is for widow."

"Thank you," I said, smiling. I untied my sash and positioned it quickly to the right.

The carousel-like beer tents beckoned, each one more extravagant than the last. Augustiner's tent pulsated like an irresistible siren call. The energy in the air was palpable, a joyful din of laughter, cheers, and the sweet melodies of traditional Bavarian music. But not just Bavarian music . . . Was that John Denver's "Country Roads"? Yes, yes, it was. Another crowd favorite was Neil Diamond's "Sweet Caroline," during which we detected a slight v for the w sounds as the crowd sang along.

I've been inclined to believe they never vould.

"Do you think we ever would have gone to Oktoberfest if we hadn't moved abroad?" I shouted to Michael, then sipped from my stein.

"I don't know," Michael replied. "But it's pretty clear that we have a lot to learn." He peered around the red-and-white tent. "What do you think everyone we know is doing on a Tuesday?"

"They aren't drinking beer at Oktoberfest!" I laughed. "I think we made the right decision." I set down the glass stein, still full. No matter how hard I'd tried, I hadn't developed a taste for beer.

At every momentous life event, I've asked myself, Am I doing the right thing? The question isn't so much about whether I've made the wrong choice, but about what other choices I could have made. What more could my future hold? I'd stepped back to wonder whether I should get married, buy a house, or get a dog. And now, standing among thousands of people from all over the world, celebrating life with beer and merriment, I checked in with myself once again: Should we have moved to Germany?

The answer was clear. Yes. A resounding yes. Despite the challenges and the uncertainty, we were exactly where we were meant to be. We were discovering a new version of ourselves in this foreign land, a version we probably wouldn't have found if we'd stayed in our familiar surroundings.

Michael and I got up and danced as the band yet again played "Ein Prosit," the iconic song of Oktoberfest. It starts with the band repeating the words "ein Prosit der Gemütlichkeit," which means "a toast to well-being."

"Those lederhosen look good on you," I said as Michael spun me around.

"Good." He beamed. "Now I won't need to buy another pair of shorts the whole time we live here."

Denied

We had been living in Heidelberg, Germany, for three months now, and I'd started to relax into our new life. I knew where the grocery store was. I had a bike. And a helmet. We now had an apartment—a huge relief after living in a tiny hotel for six weeks with two dogs and four suitcases and no refrigerator.

Most of our meals had consisted of peanut butter and jelly sandwiches. We'd bought bread, local cherry jelly, and were shocked to find creamy peanut butter after being warned that it didn't exist in Europe. Most nights we'd pull out a towel from the hotel bathroom to protect the light green duvet as we ate on our bed, discussing what we'd learned about Germans that day.

"They don't smile much, do they?" I'd ask.

"No, but they sure know how to bake bread," Michael said. "This is delicious."

One evening, after we realized we were out of peanut butter and dog food, we headed to a grocery store a couple of tram stops from the hotel. But when we arrived, the windows were dark and no one was inside. It looked like they were closed for renovations, maybe. We set off for another grocery store nearby, but that one was closed too.

Um, were we in some sort of Twilight Zone? Nope, turns out we were just in Germany. Our first lesson in German culture: all shops are closed on Sundays. The Ladenschlussgesetz was a federal law stating that retail stores had to close on Sundays and Christian holidays.

Really hungry now, we wandered until we found a German restaurant. We ordered schnitzel and Käsespätzle, which, to me, was like a heightened version of macaroni and cheese. Except the noodles were made from potatoes and the milk in the cheese came from the happiest cows on earth. I laughed, remembering what my former coworker had said about German food.

"We need to find a place to live," Michael said, picking up his beer stein.

The day after we'd arrived, we set out to find an apartment and reapply for visas to live legally in Germany. But it had been nearly two weeks and we hadn't found any promising leads on an apartment. We learned that we had to have a residence permit to apply for a visa. So we really, really needed somewhere to live.

Michael researched every Immobilien website in Heidelberg in search of a real estate agent.

I didn't know what the rental process would be like, but I was unprepared for the sheer madness of finding a home. Large groups often arrived at viewings, sometimes dozens of people, a gaggle of us following the rental agent like geese through the apartment. By the end, before we even had a chance to translate "We would like to live here," the apartment had already been snapped up. Did everyone else not need a minute to discuss the pros and cons? Or was it just that competitive?

But for one apartment viewing, we were the only ones who showed up. Curious.

A husband and wife were renting out the space; they lived next door.

"Turn the lights off by twenty-one, no more," the husband instructed us by way of greeting.

"We will know if you don't," his wife added with a smile, but her lips curled over her teeth in a way that made it feel more like a threat.

The size of this apartment could rival the Keebler Elves' miniscule tree house. The wife sat out for the tour because more than four people would have overwhelmed the space. The oven was a toaster and the microwave served as a coffee table. Hard pass on that rental.

We quickly learned that German apartments came with their own unique set of quirks. Some of them didn't even have kitchens. You had to bring your own. I couldn't help but picture us rolling up to our new place with a stove and a fridge strapped to our backs like suburban sherpas.

"I think we should switch hotels," Michael said after another failed apartment attempt and another PB&J dinner.

"Why?" I asked. The thought of moving to another temporary place sounded like a waste of time and effort.

"I found a place that's cheaper and actually larger."

I narrowed my eyes. "Can I see the reviews?"

Michael was sort of aloof when it came to determining whether something was an acceptable place to stay. He didn't want to stay in a roach-infested motel, but sometimes he could let cleanliness and amenities slide for the right price.

"There's also a park nearby where we could take the dogs," he said.

From our current hotel, we had to walk down six flights of stairs to take the dogs out to a tiny patch of grass that faced the Witter auto shop, and the scent of fumes was getting to me.

After being in the B&B Hotel for two weeks, we moved over

to Hotel Kranich, pronounced like chronic. We nicknamed it the Kranich-cles of Narnia, because it certainly was like entering a different world.

Inexplicably, a mannequin stood in the front window of the hotel entrance. She wore a short black bob wig and a smart business suit. Oh, and sensible two-inch black pumps. We named her Helga.

The front entrance was painted highlighter yellow and boasted a collection of dusty fake plants. There was a crystal bowl full of candy that I imagined had been there since the nineties, and not a single piece was taken since. The halls perpetually smelled like burnt meat from the gyro place next door. Along with PB&Js, gyros had quickly become cheap, easy meals we'd already come to love.

Our rooms were nearly double in size compared to the B&B Hotel, which made it easier to find our stuff, but the bed was rock-hard. It felt like something Fred Flintstone might prefer.

But the oddest part, save for Helga the mannequin, was the toilet, which had a shelf in it. So, when you went to the bathroom, there sat your business until you flushed. Was this for inspecting one's poop? We couldn't figure it out. The issue was, no matter what, the toilet always smelled. It also contained hardly any water. This wasn't something I'd thought much about before, but now it was glaringly obvious. There were also two buttons for the toilet, a bigger one and a smaller one, which is really quite genius. You use the bigger one if you need to flush more.

These were all things, we realized, that you often overlooked if you were only traveling to a place, not living in it.

So we continued our apartment search, eager to leave the mannequin and the shelf toilet behind.

After a dozen failed apartment viewings—we'd left the last one after learning that the neighbor had poisoned the dogs—Michael decided to go out on his own to search for apartments while I worked on my blog. He texted me to say that he'd found an ideal apartment in the perfect location.

A few hours later he returned.

"We didn't get it," Michael said sulkily.

I let out a huff and pulled my computer screen toward me to search for new listings.

I didn't notice he had one hand behind his back. "Just kidding!" He pulled out a celebratory bottle of wine. "Sorry, I had to. You won't believe this place. It's perfect."

I screamed with delight. I hadn't even seen it, but the location was exactly where I wanted to be. And I didn't care about much else. We had a place to live!

"And guess what?"

"Hmm?" I asked, pouring the wine into white coffee cups.

"We can move in immediately."

The next day, we left Hotel Kranich, and Helga the mannequin, for good. We scooped up our only belongings, four suitcases and two dogs, and hopped in a taxi to our new place.

We didn't have a bed to sleep on. No silverware, no plates, no toilet paper, no chairs, and no couch. Luckily, Michael had brought our roll-up inflatable mattresses. We immediately signed up for German Amazon Prime.

With our visa status pending, I sat on the wood floor, my back against the bare white walls, and emailed the immigration office. Hello! We officially have a residence!

Sure, the apartment was a little strange. The ceilings on the second floor were lower than those on the ground floor. Michael had to duck his head before entering our bedroom and the shower. Our windows on the second floor were all at feet level and came up to our knees. But they still let in natural light, and we didn't care—we finally had a place to live.

After staying in a hotel for weeks, I knew I could never be nomadic. Even with a thirst for traveling the world, I needed a place to come home to.

While our internet was being installed, I headed into town to get some work done. I passed by the park where we took the dogs, the Neckarwiese, where people and geese share an open patch of green lawn, and I smiled at the beauty all around. The castle stood above the town, and neat rows of manicured flowers lined the streets; it looked like a scene from a Monet painting.

I walked along the concrete bridge that connected where we lived, Neuenheim, to Heidelberg. Neuenheim is a village of Heidelberg, with amazing sandstone archways and imposing multistory mansions that had once been single-family homes but were turned into multifamily residences. This enclave is older than the city of Heidelberg itself, dating back to the thirteenth century. Most of the medieval buildings have since been destroyed, but I'd come to appreciate the lovely Gothic tower of the old St. John the Baptist church in the square where the biweekly market took place.

The architecture was so different from anything back home in Dallas, where there were definitely no castles and the oldest thing was a Tex-Mex restaurant called Mariano's, which opened in the 1920s and was famous for inventing the frozen margarita. But after three weeks of living in Germany, I was getting the hang of things. I even waved and greeted passersby with "Morgen," though I was usually met with glares. Germans don't do a lot of waving.

I popped into a quaint café, eyeing the freshly baked pastries behind the glass, and took a seat in a quiet corner. I opened my laptop. Upon checking my email, one message caught my eye. It was from a heidelberg.de email address, so I knew it was important. The email was written in German, so I pasted its contents into Google Translate.

Good day, it read. The visa applications were rejected on October 20, 2016, as no economic interest or regional need can be identified. Therefore, there are currently no prerequisites for issuing a residence permit.

That was it. Two lines told me our visas were denied. I suddenly lost my appetite for pastries.

But we'd just gotten an apartment! A bike! A helmet, for crying out loud. We were just now getting settled, and our visa was denied? Would we need to leave the country? Immediately?

I focused on steadying my trembling hands as they hovered over the keyboard. What should our next move be? Americans were allowed to stay only three months in the Schengen Area, the world's largest visa-free zone, which included Germany, France, and more than twenty other countries in Europe. After ninety days, you had to leave.

How could this happen? We'd meticulously planned every detail. Could everything come crashing down from a two-line email?

Worst of all, would I prove everyone right and come back home to Dallas, with my tail between my legs?

I called Michael.

"Listen," I said, "our visas got denied." I explained the email, trying not to let my voice catch. I felt like I couldn't breathe.

"Oh shit," Michael responded. He always kept his cool. But today was different.

We sat on the phone in silence for a few moments. I heard Hugo bark.

But then Michael said, renewed confidence in his voice, "We will figure it out. We have to."

I breathed again. We'd been determined enough to move here in the first place. We could figure this out.

In All Seriousness

The police were at our front door.

"We are here for a noise disturbance, Frau Sula," the officer said kindly but firmly.

The reason? Hugo was barking too loudly. We had been down the street grabbing one-euro scoops of gelato when our upstairs neighbor called the cops. She didn't like Hugo. I'm not sure she liked anyone, really.

We were on the bottom floor, she was on the top, and the guy in the middle, Markus, agreed with our assessment: "She can be really tough."

Markus was an impeccable dresser with a penchant for online shopping—we noticed that he received a package in the mail nearly every day. He also had a different girl at his house every few nights. Was he a gigolo? we wondered, but he seemed nice enough.

Sundays in Germany, Markus told us, were quiet days, and we—well, Hugo—had gone too far. We looked down at Hugo, who cocked his head and looked up at us in disbelief. He'd certainly done nothing wrong. Meanwhile, Millie looked on disdainfully, as if she'd already told him to be quiet three times.

Verboten is German for "forbidden," and it's one word we learned—and heard—often.

Vacuuming on Sundays? Verboten!

Idling your car? Verboten!

Washing your car at home? Verboten!

Bringing your bike on a tram? Sometimes . . . verboten! We learned that one the hard way. At certain times of day, when it's busy during the morning and afternoon commutes, you can't bring your bike on the tram. We got on a half-full tram at nearly ten in the morning and heard a man screeching, "VERBOTEN!" at us over and over. Even though he wasn't on our tram, he wanted us to know we were doing the wrong thing. It was clear that many Germans appreciated the rules and relished enforcing them.

And a dog barking too loudly—well, that was verboten too.

However, you could drive as fast as you wanted on the autobahn, and children—sixteen-year-olds—could legally drink. They did so, openly and often, in the park where we walked the dogs three times a day. Their discarded glass bottles were picked up the next day by eager recyclers, who'd pile them into bags and turn them into the recycling bins at the grocery store, earning ten to fifty cents per bottle.

As it had turned out, we were verboten too. We'd just been starting to get the hang of life abroad—strapping on our backpacks and walking or biking nearly everywhere, a glorious way to immerse ourselves in our new city—when our visas were denied. Since receiving that two-line email, we'd hired a lawyer to help us navigate the German legal system.

But I felt like a fraud. Had I really, truly moved abroad if I didn't even have a visa to live in this country? Friends and new followers would comment *Your life is goals!* and *You're living the dream!* on social media. But those comments began to feel like a gut-punch, reminding me of what I hadn't yet accomplished.

We'd moved to Germany with the intention of traveling around Europe. But so far, we had taken only a few short trips. I was too afraid to stop working on the blog to leave, even for a few days, and I was doing weekly meetings with ProSocial Business, a free program supporting start-up businesses, to work on a plan for my blog.

And now we had the visa issue to contend with. What if everything I'd been working toward as a content creator came crashing down? Then we'd have to move back!

So every morning, I returned to my black IKEA desk, where I had to lean down to see out of the low-lying half windows in the apartment, and got to work.

I took the fifteen-minute train ride to Mannheim, a larger town west of Heidelberg on the Rhine, to meet with my assigned ProSocial Business representative, Claudia, who was stern, helpful, and straightforward. She always wore black or navy trousers and a striped shirt. She printed business plans from other expats who had start-ups in Germany, and we'd meticulously comb through them for inspiration for mine. I needed to show profits from my business from the past three years, plus future income and expenses predicted for the next three.

Our goal was to create a new business plan to prove to the immigration office that Michael and I had a reason to live in Germany, under the freelance visa program.

But so far, I felt like everything I did was verboten!

Something else I noticed about Germans: they tended to take a serious approach to many things.

Our lawyer, my rep at ProSocial Business, and even the grocery store staff all had serious demeanors and prioritized efficiency over cordiality.

Once when I was in Aldi, our local grocery store, I had some extra time, so I perused the aisles, seeing what oddities I might come across. I found a blow-up hair dryer that fit around your head, a squatting stool for using the bathroom, and roach poison next to peanut butter. Yum.

I was walking up the aisle with a black plastic grocery basket in the crook of my arm when a woman approached me, speaking German.

"I'm so sorry—I don't understand. Can you speak English?" I asked. I was taking German classes and knew the basics, but I couldn't follow her fast cadence.

"Of course," she said, quickly switching over to English. "Are you okay?" She furrowed her brow and pointed at her mouth.

I wiped my lips and looked at my hand. Was I bleeding? "Yes," I said, smiling, "I'm fine."

"Okay, it's your smile. It looks kind of crazy."

"Oh" was all I could say.

It wasn't that Germans were angry or unkind. But in public, they were more austere and treated strangers more formally. My toothy grin in the grocery store came across as out of place, and even unnerving.

More and more, I began to notice cultural aspects that exemplified the practical nature of Germans. Things in Germany had sensible names, such as the town of Handschuhsheim, which meant "Hand Shoe Village." The town used to sell gloves, and gloves in Germany are sensibly called "hand shoes." Germans were also dead serious about bread, with bakeries on every corner. Sometimes there were bakeries right next to each other, which fazed absolutely no one.

Germans were often methodical, and they followed the rules. They paused to cross the street, staring fixedly at the white letters instructing them to wait, until the little green man—the Ampelmännchen—lit up and told them it was safe to walk. They never jaywalked, even if it was pouring rain and no cars were around.

Drivers were known to be skilled, cautious, and predictable. All the rule-following had a lot of benefits. Kids had free rein. They biked solo or in clusters of three or four, hanging out in parks without any parents around.

Germans were also serious about their time—something I deeply admired. Sundays weren't just quiet days; they were days to explore and go into the woods or spend time with friends and family.

I knew Europeans had far more time off than Americans, but now I really understood. It seemed as if we had a holiday every other week. Coming up next was Herbstfest, an autumn festival in the Old Town that included an open-air concert and Federweisser, or "new wine," a cloudy white wine made from grapes that were picked early.

In our neighborhood, we made it a habit to attend the biweekly market that had some of the best and freshest food I'd ever had. And it was inexpensive! Flowers from Italy, cheese from France, local sausages. Every Wednesday and Saturday, we'd head to the market for peonies the size of a small child; Galet de la Loire, a soft, strong cheese; a tub of olives; an assortment of fruit; and soft, salty pretzels the size of your head. Then we'd meander over to the sausage stand, where Michael would talk with Sausage Michael, the vendor. He had rosy-red cheeks and wore a white apron stretched taut across his ample belly. He laughed at everything. Sausage Michael gave us tips on things to eat and what to do in the area. He went out of his way to greet us and explain the different sausages.

Truthfully, we were thrilled that German culture was so different. That's why we moved to Germany in the first place. We sought out a place that wouldn't be like home. The food, the people, the customs, the environment . . . they were all different, and wonderfully so.

Above all, we'd learned that Germans were kind and sincere. They didn't say things they didn't mean, so you knew where you stood. And I seriously wanted to stay!

I just had to find a way to prove it.

An Apple in Strasbourg

Everything looked French. The people carrying messenger bags slung over their shoulders with a baguette sticking out the top. The cafés lazily strewn with chairs facing out toward the streets. Young couples vigorously making out on benches.

As I stepped off the bus, I noticed that even a cricket seemed to lean back on his haunches, observing the world going by. He just needed a beret and a cigarette to complete the look.

I was in France for the first time since moving abroad, even though we'd been in Europe for months and it took only an hour-and-a-half bus ride from Heidelberg to get there. That, I realized, was a weird way to convey the proximity, at least in Europe. Europeans tell you the distance in measurements; Americans tell you in the amount of time it takes to travel from one place to the next. So, 140 kilometers, or an hour-and-a half drive, whichever you prefer.

I was in France because I'd fried my laptop. I'd been so hyper-fixated on working on my blog that, while washing the dishes, I propped up my laptop near the sink so I could continue reading while scrubbing away. Which proved idiotic. Obviously. I spilled water on the keyboard and swore I could hear it sizzle in distress. I was desperate to get it fixed so I could start working again.

As it turned out, the closest place with an appointment for a MacBook was Strasbourg, France. I still hadn't wanted to travel very much since we'd moved. I felt tethered to my desk, working until late each evening to ensure the blog could be profitable.

For as long as I can remember, I've been obsessed with keeping count. At all my jobs, I kept a tally of something: sales, calls made, or my email-response rate. I immediately ordered a Fitbit when they came out so I could see how many steps I was taking each day. I used the Weight Watchers point system to track what I was eating. On the blog, I'd check stats every few hours to monitor where traffic was coming from. But Instagram ushered in a new level of obsession. Every ten minutes or so I'd refresh to see how many likes and comments I'd gotten. I explained it away in my head as "work." But I knew I was losing myself in something that felt more comfortable and manageable to me than actually leaving the house. Checking my stats compulsively meant that I was ensuring things wouldn't fall apart.

If I was honest with myself, it was more than that. I'd lost my routine, so I desperately clung to things I could control: the blog, taking the dogs for a walk, going shopping at the grocery store. I was hesitant to actually do what we moved to Germany for in the first place: travel.

My debilitating fear of failing kept me cloistered in our apartment. I relied on Michael to figure out everything. He'd even booked this appointment.

But now that my laptop wouldn't turn on, it was time to get out of the house and get it fixed. I was stepping out on my own, alone, in a different country. I really didn't want to get lost.

I hopped on a neon-green FlixBus and made my way to the city. Armed with my passport and a few essentials, I pressed as close as I could against the tinted window as we neared the border of the Rhine River. In Texas, I could drive twelve whole hours (or about 600 miles, 965 kilometers if you prefer) and still be in Texas. Now I could take a bus to another country in less than two hours.

"French people are so rude," countless people back home had told me. But that hadn't been my experience. I'd only ever been to Paris, and to me, Parisians just seemed busy. Kind of like how New Yorkers are busy. People move quickly, bustling by, maybe uttering short responses if prompted. It's a city in a hurry.

I get it. I often get offended by Michael when he's in a hurry and he doesn't take a moment to cover me in platitudes when he's in a rush. And I get my feelings hurt.

But there was not even a whiff of rudeness in Strasbourg. Instead I found an interesting fusion of French and German culture. Strasbourg, now part of the Alsace region of France, used to be ruled by Germany but became part of France in 1918, at the end of World War I. But, since it sits on the border of the two countries, it's heavily influenced by both cultures: I heard German and French spoken, and there are French bakeries and pastry, cheese, and wine shops, but also German shops selling sausages and restaurants offering spätzle and sauerkraut.

"Ahh, bonjour," a shopkeeper said to me, rolling up the blinds of her windows as I passed by.

"Umm, bone-jour!" I said with a wave, noticing my own slight Texas accent.

As I meandered toward the Apple store, the more commercial and industrial buildings faded into storybook half-timbered structures made of stucco in pastel colors, each with a pitched roof. I passed by adorable hotels and shops selling hand-painted ceramics and stuffed animal storks. I passed by winstubs, wine lounges that offered rich wood rooms with intimate tables and low ceilings. The city looked like something out of medieval times. In reality, I realized, it was just that.

Suddenly the narrow cobblestone street opened to a square. I craned my neck up, up, up to a gothic cathedral. I grabbed a pamphlet: "Strasbourg's Cathédrale Notre-Dame was the world's tallest building during the Middle Ages." Well, that makes sense. With my laptop under my arm, I stepped inside. The exterior of the cathedral was delicate and intricate, like a lace doily made of stone. But the interior was filled with stained glass, with a huge, gilded organ and a rose window that gave it a delicate glow. The astronomical clock struck, and a parade of wooden figures wound their way through the clock like cuckoos. I couldn't believe this was only an hour and a half from me, and it had taken breaking my laptop for me to explore it.

Following the map, I came upon a palatial open square encircled by gorgeous light-toned buildings from various time periods and architectural styles. A low fountain bubbled in the center, and a bronze statue of Kléber, the man who the square was named for, sneered down at me from his plinth as if to say, Why are you just now coming to France?

But where was the Apple store?

Oh, there it was—in the grand pink stone building that looked more like a palace. And maybe it was? The Aubette was a baroque colonnade with arched windows and carvings of faces etched into its sides, topped with the sort of rounded windows you might see on a ship. There, beneath one particularly expressive profile, was the Apple logo.

"This is their Apple store?" I wondered aloud.

I needed to get out more.

After dropping off my laptop to a very kind and helpful French man who definitely was not rude, I checked my watch. I had just enough time to catch the bus back to Heidelberg. But the light filtering through the trees was just too magnificent. I smelled freshly baked bread coming from somewhere. Screw it, I was staying.

"Michael," I said to him on the phone. "I'm staying in Strasbourg until the last bus back at ten p.m."

"Good." I could practically hear his smile. "You must be having fun."

I was buzzing with energy. I pulled up a digital map of Strasbourg and headed toward the Petite France neighborhood, where I could see a little island. I turned a corner, walked through the breezy willow trees, and stopped in the middle of the street. You know that otherworldly, angelic chorus sound effect in a movie—the one that signifies the lightbulb moment of clarity when time seems to stand still, and everything freezes in place? This happened to me. Except there really was music playing.

The scene before me looked like it came straight out of a postcard: situated at the bend in the river, a man with a fedora was playing the violin while birds flew overhead, and the still, clear water in the canal perfectly mirrored the gingerbread-like facades. The bridge was lined with beds of pink and red flowers—so many, I was astonished that the bridge hadn't collapsed into the river.

I held up my phone and quickly snapped a photo, wrote a caption, and posted it to Instagram. I tucked my phone back into my bag as if it were contraband: incompatible with the atmosphere I was living in at the moment.

As the music swirled around me, I ventured over to a nearby bakery, ogling the pastries displayed behind the large windows. I bought a croissant and found a bench. I pulled the croissant out of the brown wax bag and took a bite. Now I really was in heaven. It was the single best pastry I'd ever had in my life. Perfectly flaky and buttery. This is what food should taste like.

France—and these incredible croissants—was at my fingertips. But I'd been so consumed with worry about making our life work abroad, I'd forgotten to actually live. I was letting my fear of failing control my life. I walked back into the warm light of the streetlamps, through the tapestry of half-timbered houses. Each one, I'm sure, had a storied past.

As I pulled out my phone to check the bus schedule, I realized I had spent the whole day not refreshing my stats on Instagram. In fact, I'd barely glanced at my phone the whole day. And while I'd been busy exploring, nothing had come crashing down. The sky hadn't fallen; my blog had kept trucking along. My fear was unreasonable. I could step away from my electronics and actually experience the world.

But now I was actually a bit lost. Surely, Google Maps would point me in the right direction . . . eventually. I kept walking, and there was Rue Sainte-Hélène. My mouth hung open. Helene is a name I never see. It's never on key chains at souvenir stores (I know—I check) and people always say it wrong (they call me Helen or Helena). So, seeing my name on a street was . . . pleasantly shocking.

I used to fear getting lost. But sometimes, miraculously, you end up right where you're supposed to be.

Back on the bus, I finally checked my Instagram post from earlier that day. It was now my most-liked post ever, and it had been shared hundreds of times. Was this a hoax?

I texted Michael. Is this real?

Of course, Helene, he responded. It's a terrific photo. The caption is even better. You can tell you're really experiencing the city around you. I'm proud of you.

I thought moving abroad would change me. And it had. But I still had to create my own momentum for that change.

I really needed to get out more.

Pumpkin Head

We were heading to the largest pumpkin festival in the world, in Ludwigsburg, Germany, and I was dressing the part.

I slipped on tall brown riding boots, black leggings, a cream camisole, and a long burnt-orange cardigan. I topped the look off with a red plaid scarf and a wide-brimmed felt hat. The only thing I was missing was the Starbucks pumpkin spice latte. I had just received a comment on Instagram that had made me question who I was and what I was doing with my life. So I was going back to the basics—even stereotypical basic.

I'd posted a photo Michael had snapped of me on the bridge over the Neckar, in front of Heidelberg Castle. I was wearing a thick gray sweater and jeans.

"You look like a dumb, ugly American," the comment read, as if glaring at me through the screen. "Why did you visit Germany just to prove you know that it's more than just Italy and France? Your an idiot."

Despite my better judgment, I engaged with this grammatically challenged commenter: "Actually, I live here."

"Great," they typed back. "Another fat American making us look bad. Move back."

The rational part of my brain knew this comment didn't matter, but I couldn't stop dwelling on it.

Now I scrutinized my reflection over and over in the mirror, trying to figure out how to look put together without trying too hard. I pulled off the scarf and stuffed it in my bag.

Michael, on the other hand, had the whole "not caring" part down.

He blissfully ignored fashion trends and what was posted on social media. He simply didn't care. Most of his shirts had holes, he used a pink phone case because it was the cheapest he could find, and he wasn't bothered when someone flipped him off on the freeway. He'd wave back with a peace sign. He will dance—albeit poorly—on the dance floor with abandon, just enjoying himself.

Michael is, to me, one of the finest human beings on Earth. He's frugal when it comes to spending money on himself but overly generous when it comes to tipping. He opens doors, visits friends in the hospital, mows a neighbor's lawn while they're away. He's a great cook and he likes to clean.

He's far less frustrated than most people I know because he resigns himself to care only about things that actually matter. Maybe he's gotten even more unconcerned with the small stuff since his mother died, but he's also always been this way. He just isn't rattled easily. Meanwhile, I become ruffled at the slightest breeze. We even each other out.

So when I told him that someone had called me ugly and dumb on the internet, his response bothered me.

"Well, isn't that a good thing? Anyone who's anyone has haters," he concluded.

But the Instagram comment still stung.

"Look, Helene," Michael continued as we drove to Ludwigsburg, "if you're going to put yourself out there, you're going to have to deal with the fact that not everyone will like you."

"I understand that," I said, picking at my nails. "I just don't know what my looks have to do with it. I feel like maybe I shouldn't share at all."

Publicly, I still hid the fact that we hadn't secured a visa yet, as I wasn't sure, legally, what I could share. This negative comment seemed to reinforce my doubts about sharing anything.

"Of course you should share. You know that." He shook his head. "I believe you're the one teaching people that if they don't take a chance and tell their story, they'll never know what life could look like."

"You're right." Regret would fester more than that comment. I rewrapped my scarf around my neck and glided on some lipstick.

"They sound like a pumpkin head," he said, trying to make me laugh. I cracked a sliver of a smile.

Our feet crunched through brown leaves under a canopy of bare trees leading up to the grounds. We could hear a live orchestra playing in the distance; we quickened our pace, hoping not to miss it.

It was clear this was no ordinary pumpkin patch. The Ludwigsburg Pumpkin Festival was held on the grounds of a gleaming canary-yellow palace. Pumpkins weren't just spilling out on the ground; they had been carved into birds, clowns . . . Even entire words had been spelled out in pumpkins.

This year's theme was the circus, replete with pumpkin archways and animals. Everywhere we turned, pumpkins of every size, shape, and color greeted us—from tiny, cute pumpkins to massive, jaw-dropping giants. How on earth had they managed to grow so big? But to me, the most impressive part of the festival was the creativity of the pumpkin carvings and sculptures: live on the spot, artists etched detailed faces, complete with lifelike lines, evocative eyes, and furrowed brows, into the flesh of pumpkins.

We discovered pumpkin-flavored soups, pastries, and even pumpkin-infused drinks, including wine.

"Screw it," I said. "Michael, take a picture of me holding this pumpkin."

I chose a sizable classic orange pumpkin, heaved it up, and stood in front of the display of circus animals, the baroque palace on the hill above serving as my backdrop. I wasn't going to let one nasty comment stop me from sharing my experiences.

We spent the rest of the day touring the castle grounds and geometric gardens, eating and drinking pumpkin-flavored everything, and visiting the summer residence Schloss Favorite, which happened to be the color of a pumpkin, with bright orange balustrades and stone vase statues.

The next morning, I woke up in our hotel room and pulled my own, separate comforter over my head. A king bed in Germany is two beds pushed together, no top sheet, with individual duvets. I was starting to like it. The dogs continued snoring undisturbed, the room still completely dark from the blackout Rolladen, metal rolling shades that blocked out both light and cold.

I often woke up without an alarm. Michael is a very light sleeper, so I tucked my head under the covers and checked Instagram, then opened Gmail.

The subject line "Paid collaboration to go to . . ." immediately snagged my attention.

I sat bolt upright, the covers flying off me and immediately disturbing the dogs. When the dogs wake up, they don't do it half-assed. They wake up and start tap dancing around as if it's Christmas morning and if we don't hurry up, Santa might actually take back our presents.

Suddenly everyone was awake.

"What is it, Helene?" Michael groaned, removing his eye mask.

"I got an offer for a paid collaboration . . . from a real company!" I squealed, then scanned the email. "They want to pay me! To travel!" I was singing, dancing around the room just like the dogs.

Could this be? Was it possible to get paid to travel? The trip wasn't until the spring of 2017, months and months from now. But that didn't matter.

Michael lifted me up and kissed me on the forehead. "Wow. Helene, wow! This is big. Huge."

"W-wow," I said, barely able to speak. "I really hope we get our visa approved." I lay back down in bed, in our red-and-white hotel room, envisioning it all: getting paid to travel. To create itineraries, experiences—on my own terms.

"How did they hear about you anyway?" Michael asked.

I scanned the email further, smiling. "Instagram."

It felt like a whole new world had just opened up. I had simply never heard of people getting paid to travel, not unless they were real journalists. So what did that make me? I didn't know. All I knew was that I could get paid to do something I loved, something I'd once thought was reserved only for beautiful fashion bloggers and Instagram models.

I didn't have a guide or reference for this. There was no map to give me step-by-step directions. I felt dazed, but mostly I felt determined. This was a breakthrough. I hadn't known it until it was staring back at me in an email. But I wanted a way to get paid to travel.

Not long ago I'd thought my life was going one way. I had it all planned out. And I never expected to make a career out of sharing about my travels. But now I was set on continuing to post on social media and create blogging courses, trolls be damned.

I thought about the girl who'd been afraid to leave home, who was really just scared of changing her surroundings. I'd been so worried that if things in my life changed too much, I'd lose myself. I was still that girl, but I was ready to take a risk and venture into the unknown. And I could just be myself.

Friendship Cookies

Don't wear white to a haunted house. Unless, of course, you want to be picked out of a crowd. Personally, I never want to be picked on. Maybe the only exception would be if the lead actress in *Mamma Mia!* twisted her ankle on stage and I'm in the audience—in which case, I am completely ready to fill in for the role.

It was my second time ever going to a haunted house. The first time was my senior year of high school, when Michael dragged me along on a date. I've never been able to stomach horror movies, and I knew haunted houses just weren't my thing. But I was trying to be brave in front of this new guy I was dating.

"And the people working—they can't touch you, right?" I checked with Michael.

"Correct. Legally, they cannot touch you." He smiled and held my hand.

At the haunted house, set in an abandoned warehouse outside of Dallas, Michael took the first opportunity to disappear into the darkness and then pop out at me like a demented jack-in-the-box. I nearly punched him in the face.

Now we were on a train headed to a Halloween party at Frankenstein Castle. The real one that Mary Shelley wrote about in Frankenstein.

Before we left, we went over to a fellow expat's apartment for drinks. Shaun was a British student who we'd met at a pub quiz in our neighborhood. He and his girlfriend, Anna, who was German, had told us about the Halloween party, inviting us to their place before taking the train to Frankenstein Castle.

Nervous and excited to meet up with some potential new friends, I wanted to make a good first impression, so I made chocolate chip cookies from scratch. The first batch was thin and lopsided, looking more like crackers—I got the measurements mixed up because I was still struggling with the metric conversions. The second batch was more like cake. But by the third batch, I'd gotten it right.

I donned my fuzzy half-snap-up Patagonia sweater and jeans, and we biked over to Shaun's apartment on the Hauptstrasse, locking up our bikes on a lamp pole where the warm light glowed over their silver, metal frames.

"Can you take off your shoes?" Shaun said when he cracked the door open. He wore bifocals with a distinct line across the glass, and I noticed he was balding on the top of his head. He looked like a young Benjamin Franklin.

Taking off your shoes before entering someone's home wasn't as common in America, but in every house in Germany, it was a requirement. Since we'd bought nearly all our furniture from sellers on Craigslist, we'd gotten used to walking around in socks in strangers' homes.

"Is anyone else here?" I asked Michael as I kicked off my white tennis shoes.

"I don't know, maybe," he replied, then straightened up and opened the door the rest of the way.

You wouldn't have guessed it from outside, but there were nearly a dozen or so guests in the room, all holding glasses of wine. It had been so quiet, I could have heard a mouse eating cheese in the next room.

"Hello," I said, going up to Shaun. "Thanks for inviting us! I brought cookies."

"Oh," Shaun said shyly, glancing around the room. "Hand them to Anna; she'll know what to do with them."

"Hi, Anna," I said, lowering my voice; I'd realized I was the loudest in the room. "I'm Helene. I made chocolate chip cookies!"

"You made these?' she asked, inspecting the cookies. "I have a better recipe."

She took the cookies and whisked them away, hiding them behind the nuts and chips. I stood in place, unsure if she was serious and I should laugh.

"This is like trying to make friends with cats," I said, leaning into Michael and scanning the room.

"Tough crowd," he mumbled out the side of his mouth.

I'd always considered myself an extrovert. In school, I was loquacious and willing to talk to anyone about nearly anything. But when we moved to Germany, I realized that I'd always existed in a safe bubble surrounded by friends. My own husband was from my high school, and I hadn't really made a friend who wasn't linked to one of my other friends since the first grade. Now making friends was proving more difficult, and I felt more cautious when striking up a conversation.

My cookies lay uneaten on the table.

Michael grabbed a few. "These are delicious, Helene! And still warm."

"I think that's because of the temperature in here." I took one too.

The room really was contemptuously warm, the radiator only blowing in more hot air. I could feel a bead of sweat trickling down the small of my back. This was something else we'd learned: Germans tended to keep their homes stiflingly warm. In our own apartment, we tried not to use our heat if we could help it; the cost for electricity was sky-high.

After the hot, quiet party, we took the forty-five-minute train ride to Darmstadt, the city just outside the castle.

As I nervously walked up toward the thousand-year-old castle, I could see the faint outline of trees of the Odenwald forest. And there, sitting atop a craggy hill, were Frankenstein Castle's imposing stone walls, turrets, and battlements, some in ruins, others intact. The castle seemed to breathe in and out as if it were alive, the blue and orange lights glowing ominously. A heavy mist crept up from the ground, solidifying the creepy atmosphere.

I felt out of place in my fuzzy white sweater. Nearly everyone was wearing black, or dark colors, and those who hadn't worn street clothes were dressed in terrifying costumes. It was hard to decipher who was an actor in the haunted house and who was just a guest. Everyone seemed to have professional makeup that was oozing either blood or green mucous. One man had managed to make it look like he had a severed head.

Suddenly I felt someone snatch my pink beanie off my head. Then two men—who looked like orcs from *The Lord of the Rings* with their coarse gray-green skin, turned-down ears, and tufts of black hair sprouting from bald skulls—laughed and picked me up and tossed me into an open coffin.

I guess they can touch you in Germany.

"Maybe next time you shouldn't wear white," Michael said, helping me out of the coffin, and I stuffed the pink puff ball beanie into my purse.

Even though I had been nearly scared to death, I thought the Halloween party was incredible. Germans take the holiday seriously and knew how to throw a party. Inside, there was a zombie rockabilly band playing American music. Every time they switched from songs like Jerry Lee Lewis's "Whole Lotta Shakin' Goin' On" to singing in German, it was like getting hit with a reality check: Oh, right—we're in Germany!

We drank an elixir of life punch, a nod to the legend that Johann Konrad Dippel, an alchemist, had concocted the potion here.

"'This is Germany's oldest and largest Halloween party,'" Michael read from a small plaque next to a large oil painting of Frankenstein hung on the stone wall.

"Of course it is," said a man as he picked carefully through his small sandwich. "Germans always let you know if it is the oldest or the best."

"How's the sandwich?" Michael gestured to the man's plate.

"Terrible." He sighed. "I'm Renault, like the French car. And, yes, I am French. You are American, yes?"

"Yes," Michael and I responded in unison.

I was thrilled he was the one who had initiated the conversation. I usually struggled to come up with much more than "What do you do for a living?" when first meeting someone—an American conversational tick. This wasn't the case in Europe. In fact, it felt borderline rude to ask questions like that right after meeting someone.

"What brought you to Germany?" I asked, pleased with myself for thinking of a different question other than his career.

"Work," he blurted casually. "I'm from Metz, but I have been here now three years. And you?"

"Moved from Texas to Heidelberg to travel more of Europe and experience another way of living," Michael said.

"Cool." Renault smiled easily. "You should check out the expat meetup group. It's how I met my girlfriend, who is also French. You'll love it."

A few days later, armed with a new batch of cookies, we headed to O'Reilly's, the neighborhood Irish pub that hosted an English-speaking comedy night for expats.

"You're bringing cookies into a bar?" Michael said, laughing.

I hugged the bag of cookies tightly to my chest. I thought they would be a good way to make conversation. And they felt a little like a security blanket. "If they don't like me, maybe they'll like the cookies," I said, making sure the Ziploc bag was secure.

We opened the worn wooden door into a tightly packed bar, with just enough room for a few tiny two-seat tables and bar stools that sallied up to the bar. We walked under the green lanterns and into a back room that opened into a second bar, with a small wooden stage, round tables seating five or six people, and tapered risers in the back to watch the show.

The comedy was abysmal. The combination of the bad jokes and the ludicrously drunk guy at our table made it hard to laugh. But I was there to make friends, not to be entertained. After the show, Michael and I milled around, looking for a group to break into, when I noticed a young guy sitting in the corner of the risers staring fixedly at Michael. He glanced away when he saw me but then turned back again. Finally he approached us.

"Excuse me," he began in an unmistakable American accent, his eyes still fixed on Michael. "Do I know you?"

I could've sworn I detected a faint Texan twang.

"I—I don't think so," Michael said, clutching his beer.

"Well, I'm Luke." He offered his hand. "I recognized your face, but your ring confirmed it."

We both looked at Michael's ring: a thick gold band bearing his university crest.

Then I looked to see the same ring on Luke's hand.

"Oh, Luke!" Recognition flashed in Michael's eyes. "I pulled your boots!" Michael turned to me. "Helene, Luke was in Outlaw 8, my same outfit in the Corps at A&M!"

Michael had been a freshman at Texas A&M when Luke was a senior. Michael explained to me that each year, seniors received handmade boots that often needed to be "pulled off" after wearing. That job was left for freshmen, and Michael had pulled Luke's.

They were immediate friends, buying each other beers and recounting the terrible days of the Corps as if sharing old war stories.

Out of a school of 73,000, they'd met again in a bar in a small town in Germany, five thousand miles from home.

I pulled out the Ziploc bag of cookies and offered one to Luke.

"Wow, you made these?" he exclaimed, smiling. "They taste like home!"

Homesick on Christmas

"Mom," I said over the phone, "I'm overwhelmed."

"Hold on, you're on speaker. Everyone, say hi to Helene!" she screamed. "We are in the car, on the way to Aunt Helene's for Thanksgiving." I was named for my aunt, and for the first time in many years, I'd be missing Thanksgiving with my family.

"Hi," I singsonged, faking a happy voice.

Mom lowered her voice. "What's wrong?"

"I just—" I broke off. "There's so much. We still don't have our visas. I'm worried about the business. Michael hates what he's doing. I never leave the apartment because I'm worried about the blog. And I'm homesick. I'm going to miss the Christmas party for the first time in my life. I'm overwhelmed."

"Well, that's a good thing," she said, her voice still low.

"What? How is this good?"

"The question is: Would you be happy doing less? Of course not." She went on to say that a full life is thick with regrets. The more we live, the more we want to be in two places at once. We can't do it all.

"Isn't that wonderful?" she said. "So just don't worry about it. Go live your life."

"Yeah, you have a point. I just don't know who will slice all the rolls and DJ the music for the party." I took my role for the Christmas party seriously.

After I got off the phone, I took to the blog and wrote about how I was feeling, detailing my family's over-the-top gumbo-themed Thanksgiving spread with three turkeys and a ragtag group of seventy family members from across the country to spend the holiday in Baton Rouge, Louisiana. Would I ever be able to find that kind of community abroad?

"You know," Michael said, "you can't really write much about our life abroad if you never leave the apartment to explore."

I was furious. I'm always the most furious when he's right.

We registered on Meetup and expat.com to try to make friends. The next day, I joined a writers' group.

As I biked into town, I noticed yellow stars strung between the buildings, wreaths on doors, and people setting up wooden stands. Before moving, we'd heard about Christmas markets in Europe. They'd started in Germany, and I'd been excited to see them here in Heidelberg. I'd imagined they would just be outdoor markets where vendors sold Christmas items. But that was only the start of it.

I turned down the Old Bridge and smiled up at the castle. I saw the small round sign above the door for Yilliy, locked up my bike, and walked inside, where I was greeted by the intoxicating aroma of cocoa. A harpist played softly in a corner, a fireplace warmed the space, and a line of patrons wound behind the glass case of decadent chocolates. A little sign by the register announced that they took credit cards, which was a relief, since many places in Germany were still cash only.

Before joining the line, I took a picture of the menu and put it into my Google Translate app on my phone to decipher what to order. The specials offered were Trinkschokoladen, or drinking chocolates. I sallied up to the register and said, "Trinkschokolade bitte."

The young man at the register with his hair slicked back blinked and then spoke in English: "There are fifteen varieties—which one?"

"Oh, um, whatever you like best." I tried a weak smile.

This was not the right answer. "I am not a magician. What I like you might not."

"Yes, how about dark?"

"Okay, that will be three-fifty euro," he said.

Germans all seemed to pronounce Euro like "err-yo" instead of "yur-o," like Americans pronounce it. But the way they said everything was so foreign to me, and everything I tried to say in German felt wrong. Even when I spoke to Germans in German, like this guy in the chocolate shop, they would answer in English!

I stepped aside and waited for my drinking chocolate. I scanned the room and noticed a group clustered around three or four tables near the fireplace, their laptops open as they spoke in English. When my name was called, I collected the beautiful blue-and-white ceramic cup full of hot milk and a chocolate stick and headed to the tables.

"Hello!" I said. "I'm here for the writers' group."

"Pull up a chair," said an older man with an English accent. Dressed in tweed, he was presiding over the group. "We have a couple of new members today, so we can go over the rules and how the meetings proceed."

Everyone in the circle took turns introducing themselves, noting where they were from and the premise of their book. Everyone, it seemed, was writing a novel. Except for me. I was just writing a blog. And I went last.

"I'm Helene. I'm from Texas, so my apologies if I say y'all . . . um . . . I'm a travel blogger. A travel writer." I caught a middle-aged woman with a notebook and pen rolling her eyes.

The tweed jacket man instructed us to write for the next twenty minutes, then we'd discuss. I'd already forgotten everyone's names.

"Do you like your chocolate?" a man with long hair asked me, then introduced himself as Robert. I could tell he was German from his accent.

"Oh my goodness, it's amazing. Seriously, I've never had anything like it. It's like drinking happiness." I stirred the chocolate with the spoon, the milk now a rich brown color.

He cracked a wry smile. "I don't like Americans because you lie. Everything is great or terrible. You lie a lot."

Well, that was abrupt. Was he joking?

"Well, I guess we do use a lot of superlatives," I considered. "But I don't think we are necessarily lying." I smiled, trying to act like that was a normal thing to say to someone you just met.

"And you are too loud," he continued.

"Robert, why don't you work on your science-fiction book?" a young woman a table over said. She was tall with natural blond hair and blue eyes.

I smiled at her in thanks and went back to pretending to write. I couldn't concentrate. But I wasn't really there to write anyway; I was there to make friends. Chances are, Robert wouldn't be one of them. As the meeting wrapped up, I hung behind to talk to the young woman.

"Thanks for the help earlier!" I said.

"No problem," she replied. "Germans can be really tough. I should know—I'm German." She laughed. "I'm Lisa, by the way—in case you don't remember my name, because I don't remember yours."

"Oh, good! Yes," I said, relieved. "I'm Helene. And I thought he was being a bit forward, but I guess he's right: Americans can be over the top."

"We all have our faults, each culture." She opened the door out onto the street. "Want to go for a Glühwein?" she asked.

"Are the markets open yet? I've never had one before!"

"Yes," she said brightly. "You will love it."

We made our way up the street, in the direction of the castle, toward the market. As we turned a corner, my mouth fell open. Red-and-white tents lined with twinkling lights and wreaths were selling sausages and sandwiches, steam billowing from round metal skillets as big as tables. People were milling about in thick, puffy down coats, beanies, and scarves, drinking ceramic cups full of hot mulled wine, or Glühwein. Below the castle was an ice-skating rink. The whole scene looked like a Norman Rockwell painting—if Norman Rockwell had been to a German Christmas market.

"Well, not to be an American stereotype, but this is shocking," I marveled.

"It's beautiful, right? And this isn't even the best one!" Lisa said. "The one at Universitätsplatz is my favorite. It should be up today."

"This Glühwein," I said apprehensively, not sure exactly how to pronounce it, "is amazing. I guess I thought it would taste more like wine, but it's perfectly sweet."

"Try it with a shot of rum next time," she offered.

"Oh, how do I ask for that?"

"Einen Schuss Rum bitte?" she answered.

"Thanks, I'm still working on my German—I speak almost nothing still."

"I can teach you!" she exclaimed. "I teach German."

When Lisa had to leave for work, I stayed back and called Michael.

"What are you doing?" I said when he answered.

"Just tightening up the zip ties on the fence," he said with a grunt.

For the past few weeks, he'd been building a fence around the tiny garden outside our apartment. We didn't have a car, so he would haul cement blocks in a backpack, roll up the fence material, and schlep it all to and from on a tram. He'd had to carry multiple cement blocks for over a mile because the tram stopped early that day.

"Oh, thanks for doing that," I said.

Michael was always proactive about handling our housework so I could work on my blog.

"Do you want to take a break and meet me for lunch in town at the Christmas market?" I asked.

"Be there in ten minutes," he said.

Michael met me at Universitätsplatz, and we walked hand in hand up the street. We were immediately hit with the aroma of candied nuts, hot mulled wine, and freshly cut pine. This market was even better than the last. Instead of red-and-white tents, hand-carved wooden stalls lined the streets, each one selling exquisite glass ornaments, sheepskins, or sausages roasting on large open grills. Each stall had been decorated differently: we saw ornate carvings of Santa and his reindeer, lights, wreaths, and stars.

Stalls billowed with steam as vendors poured Glühwein. At one stall we bought a half-dozen light-as-air doughnuts, dusted with powdered sugar and tossed into paper sacks for only €1.50.

"Okay, but let's get some real food too," Michael said.

We continued through the market, barely speaking, enraptured by the glow of merriment around us.

"That looks good," Michael said, pointing to a huge pan. The sizzling meat there looked like a burger, but we soon discovered that it was made of pork and topped with grilled onions and mustard.

"Eine Frikadelle bitte," Michael said to the vendor.

"Zweibel?" he asked Michael.

"Ja!" We didn't know much German, but we did know the word for onion because Michael loves onions.

Michael squeezed mustard on the burger and took a bite.

"Oh my god, you have to try this," he said between bites.

"You know I don't really like burgers," I said.

"It's not a burger—it's pork," he said, handing me the sandwich.

It was divine, tender and hearty with a mix of herbs and spices.

"I think I need one too," I swallowed.

We spent the rest of the day at the markets. Vendors were clustered in six different areas along the main street, each one with its own distinct offering.

When day turned to night, twinkling lights blazed along the streets. We sipped on Glühwein, quietly taking in the scene around us. In the glow of those lights, I forgot I missed home.

In Dallas, one of my favorite things to do around the holidays is drive around to see Christmas lights while listening to carols. Each year, Highland Park, a city in Dallas County, puts on a holiday display, with each house more extravagantly decorated than the last. Some houses have life-size figurines carved out of wood. One even features a carousel that plays Christmas music. These massive multimillion-dollar homes scream, Look how much money we have!

But Germany didn't have all this bravado. Instead of elaborate home displays, the city centers were decorated. And even during cold, rainy days, people congregated outside to drink mulled wine and eat pork sandwiches. It was different from home, but it was still wonderful.

I could feel myself taking a step back, shifting my perspective away from the commercialism of the holidays. We had no home to decorate. I would buy gifts for just Michael and the dogs. All I had to do was relax and enjoy.

Of course, I was still allowed to miss home. But Michael and I could also create new traditions—like drinking copious amounts of Glühwein and marveling at how this fairy-tale town had somehow become even more beautiful during the holidays.

I'd always thought home was the only magical place to be for Christmas. But now that I'd stepped out of my proverbial comfort zone, I realized I didn't have to celebrate Christmas the same way every year. And wherever I was, it could still be magical.

Kool-Aid Worms

A text message flashed on my screen: "I hope my visit won't add too much to your already very full plate."

Well, I wouldn't be homesick for long: my mom was coming to visit for three weeks right after Christmas.

"No," I wrote back to her. "I've realized how wonderful it is to be overwhelmed. Beats the heck out of being underwhelmed."

I've always loved Christmas, but Germany officially made me a full-blown fanatic.

Michael and I spent the holidays exploring the Christmas markets all around Germany. We went to tiny towns like the gingerbread village of Mosbach, which looked like a pop-up holiday card with its storybook half-timber buildings.

None of it would have happened without Michael. Not just the trips, not the move abroad, not even my blog. And, especially, making friends—something I desperately needed. Friends, I realized, helped to make a place feel like home.

We realized that he had a special knack for planning out our travel. He used his research skills to find inexpensive flights and lodgings, as well as the best ways to experience a new destination. While he worked out the details, I had time to work on my blog.

In an effort to get the heck out of our apartment more and experience Europe, Michael found a nine-euro flight to London leaving out of Nuremberg; we couldn't pass it up.

"I hoped we'd go someplace new," Michael said, slinging his blue backpack over his shoulder and mounting his bike.

"It will feel new. We've never seen London at Christmas! Plus, we're going to Nuremberg—that's new," I countered.

In Nuremberg, beneath an ancient Frauenkirche cathedral, we found the *real* traditional German Christmas—one of the oldest Christmas markets in the world. The stalls were set up with uniform red-and-white tents lined with garlands of lights. The vendors sold Glühwein, Lebkuchen, and Maroni—mulled wine, gingerbread, and roasted chestnuts. Comforts I thought I'd only find in a Nat King Cole song.

A woman clad in a radiant robe of white and adorned with a golden crown that shimmered like starlight handed out cookies to children. This, we learned, was Christkindl, the embodiment of the spirit of Christmas itself.

Walking around the market, we were enthralled by the abundant scene. Despite the excitement, we did our best to act like normal Christmas market goers, sipping Glühwein properly as we perused the stalls. But then we turned a corner and I shrieked with delight: a table, right there in Nuremberg, filled with Kool-Aid. We had happened upon the international Christmas market, and here was a booth labeled Atlanta, Georgia. We bought twenty or so packets, thrilled to have a small taste of home.

As the sun lowered in the sky and the twinkling lights burned brighter, a children's choir started singing beneath the cathedral spires. Everyone around us turned to watch and listen to the beautiful, haunting voices. At first I couldn't tell what the song was, but I could tell that Michael had immediately picked up the notes—he has an ear for music.

I watched his face, transfixed by the scene in front of him, and I saw a tear slowly slide down his cheek. It finally registered—the song was "Silent Night," one of his mother's favorite Christmas songs.

Michael hadn't spoken much about his mom's death. It had happened so close to our move, and we'd been so wrapped up in finding a place to live, securing our visas, and just trying to find our footing in a foreign country. He was never one to cry, and whenever I tried bringing up Jan's passing, he told me pointedly that he didn't want to discuss it. But there, under the glow of the lights, listening to the sweet voices of the children's choir, I could see he was letting himself feel for the first time.

"My mom would have loved this," Michael said, still staring ahead.

"She would have." I grabbed his hand and squeezed. "But I bet she'd be glad you're experiencing it."

"I think she'd be excited about the Kool-Aid, too." A half smile tugged at his lips.

On the flight from Nuremberg, we were utterly tickled with our luck. The nine-euro Ryanair flight was practically empty, and we splayed out in separate rows on the mustard-yellow-and-navy-blue seats.

I felt a rush of relief when we reached London. The city felt familiar and new at the same time, like an old friend you haven't seen in a while, but you pick up right where you left off. Even the pugnacious commuters packed into the Tube were gilded by my happiness of returning to a city I loved.

The best time in London is after working hours, when the windows of pubs gleam like jewels and patrons spill out onto the streets, drinking beers with open collars and removed ties.

This time of year, hordes of people milled around Oxford Street, the pubs festooned with lights, holly wreaths, and Christmas trees. Round globes of paper lanterns had been strung from the tops of buildings, and some shops had even wrapped their entire facades like presents. Huge, life-sized angels hung over the length of Regent Street as double-decker buses glided beneath. In Covent Garden, mirrored ornaments the size of a Mini Cooper hung alongside gargantuan mistletoe. Each street was more elaborate than the next. I soaked it all up. I didn't want to leave.

The day we got home, Michael reminded me that we'd planned to attend an expat event that evening.

"We have, like"—he looked at his watch—"twenty minutes."

I appreciated how respectful Michael had been of my work time, but I was starting to feel lonely without any friends in Heidelberg. In addition to my writers' group, I wanted to try to make more friends. It was time to force myself out of my little bubble.

I threw on a dress, my red coat, and gloves, and we marched out the door.

We arrived at a brightly lit restaurant that looked as if it had been dressed up like a wedding cake. Everything was white: the linens, the chairs, even the spiral staircases leading up to the InterNations meetup event.

Light appetizers were served on tiered white trays with—you guessed it—white wine. We noticed a couple scrutinizing a cracker topped with cheese and shrimp.

"Anything any good?" Michael asked them.

"No, this is terrible," the guy answered.

"In fact, everything has been pretty bad," the girl whispered conspiratorially.

We started chatting with the couple, whose names we learned were Abdul and Letizia, and we all decided to switch to a "real" restaurant. They picked an Italian place across the street.

"Letizia knows Italian—she's German but has Italian heritage," Abdul said.

Abdul was from Saudi Arabia but had lived in Canada and now in Germany; he worked for one of the largest software companies in the world. Letizia had been born in Germany, but her family was from Sicily.

Letizia's accent was a blend of a melodious Italian accent mixed with the distinct clarity of vowels only Germans seem to have mastered. She sounded like a 1920s movie star: "Ah, Helene-a, vhat do you think of the Christmas markets?" she asked. I loved her immediately.

"Oh, I adore them!" I squealed.

"Then you must go to Worms!" Letizia announced. "We will take you."

A few days later we headed to Worms—pronounced "Voms," Letizia's hometown and also where, in 1521, Martin Luther had refused to recant his beliefs, sparking the Protestant Reformation.

I couldn't wait to visit this historic city, but we were running late. Michael and I met Abdul and Letizia at their apartment, and we were waiting on one of Abdul's American friends to join us.

Letizia checked her watch. "If ve don't go now, ve vill miss it!"

We left without Abdul's friend and ran to the train station like a pack of wild hyenas, laughing as we lugged a large thermos of Glühwein toward the open doors of the train. Panting, we clutched the steel poles as the doors closed.

A freckled hand shot out, just clipping the automatic doors, and they opened again. A very sweaty young guy, whose red hair matched his crimson face, walked in, huffing. "I made it!"

Abdul clasped the man's hands, and we all let out a collective laugh. We were then introduced to Abdul's friend Eric, who hailed from North Carolina and was easygoing and kind.

It was a clear, crisp day. We passed by Martin Luther's statue as Letizia, acting as our tour guide, pointed out important buildings and monuments. Our tour ended at the Christmas market. There we met two more people, Megan and Tyler, also expats from America.

After a ride on the carousel and a hefty snack of Kartoffelpuffer (fried potatoes), we met Letizia's parents at their Italian restaurant, Kupferkessel Al Duomo. The cuisine was a mix of German and Italian, just like Letizia herself. While Letizia's father worked in the kitchen, Letizia's mother brought out dish after dish: steaming swordfish, Sicilian baked pasta, spaghetti topped with fresh parmesan and truffle shavings. Italian music played in the background. It was perfect.

Full of wine and pasta, we sat in the glow of the candlelight as the other patrons began to leave. Letizia's family—Letizia's sister and her husband and child—came out from the back of the restaurant once we were the only people left. We laughed and talked for hours.

As I looked around the room, I felt my throat tighten. I was becoming part of a family and I was creating new friendships. I hadn't known what was missing from my life, but now I knew, this was definitely it.

Marie Antoinette and Mom

My mom came to visit me in Germany in the dead of winter. Wearing a thrift store trench coat, she lugged heavy Bath & Body Works candles and a couple of jars of Clint's Texas Hot Salsa—some of the things I missed most from home—in an old suitcase with a broken wheel. She was a sight to behold.

And as soon as I saw her, I burst into tears. No person represented home more than my mom. No one else could simultaneously make me feel loved unconditionally and also a little guilty for not coming home for Christmas—all without uttering a word.

My mom is the closest thing to magic I've ever seen. She never believed in paying for things; instead she believed in maneuvering so that the universe granted her what she needed. And often, it proved true. When I was young, I desperately wanted an American Girl doll. Around the same time, my mom started writing stories for *Dallas Child* magazine. She pitched an article in which she'd review the best toys for young girls. Of course, she'd need the toys to review them properly. That Christmas, under the tree—right next to Santa's sooty footprints that were oddly the same size shoes as my dad's—was a Kirsten doll. Unwrapped and on display was her entire wardrobe, a house, and a horse. Needless to say, I certainly believed in my mother's powers.

In her late sixties, my mom still looked to be in her fifties, mostly because she didn't understand the idea of stopping or slowing down. The plan for her three-week trip was to spend the first week in Heidelberg, with day trips to surrounding cities, then zigzag through Munich, Austria, Neuschwanstein Castle in Germany, and then Switzerland. We'd end the trip in Paris for my thirtieth birthday. So, not much planned at all.

There is something special about showing your mom something you're proud of, and Michael and I were proud to show her the life we'd created in Germany. She must have forgotten, though, that we lived in a one-bedroom apartment. She and I would be sleeping on the bed, and Michael would sleep on the floor on a blow-up mattress with the dogs.

It was our first New Year's abroad, and we'd heard that Heidelberg put on a particularly impressive fireworks show above the castle. We planned to buy some sparklers and watch the show from the bridge near our apartment.

Suddenly every grocery store sold fireworks, the one time a year they were legal. They were displayed in bins next to signs reading Guten Rutsch, which translated to "good slide," as in a good slide into the next year.

As we headed toward the street, we heard high-pitched, piercing whistles followed by explosive bangs coming from every direction. The streets were like a war zone. Because while the professional fireworks show lit up the sky above the castle, amateurs stood on the bridge, blowing up anything they could find. Fireworks were shoved indecorously into gaps in ancient brickwork or in beer bottles. Some went off into the sky; others skittered into the crowd.

Police cars stood watch and ambulances had their doors open, waiting for inevitable injuries.

"Wow, this is wild," my mom observed, laughing at the general pandemonium.

One kid spotted her and immediately shot a firework directly at her head. She ducked and missed it, but I swore it nearly tinged her thrift store trench coat.

"This is like the Purge," Michael said, referring to the 2013 dystopian horror film in which citizens are allowed to commit violent crimes in a twelve-hour period once a year.

After a week in Heidelberg, we headed toward the Alps. The temperature began to steadily drop as we made our way toward the mountains, prompting my mom to buy a real coat at Galeria Kaufhof in Munich. On the way, we went to the Nazi concentration camp in Dachau, shocked that anyone could survive a winter without a coat; the disconnect between the ornate beauty of Munich and the brutal history of the concentration camp was palpable. We read about *Vergangenheitsaufarbeitung*, which means "working off the past"—referring to Germany's decades-long process of coming to terms with Nazism and the Holocaust. I was appreciative that German culture takes into account this history.

Neuschwanstein Castle was the perfect next stop after the heaviness of Dachau. Atop a blanket of snow, the white limestone of the castle stood proudly. We walked up, the snow crunching under our feet. I shared my hiking poles with my mom and we proudly climbed while others took horse-and-carriage rides. Not my mom. We laughed, thinking about mad King Ludwig of Bavaria and his perfect romantic castle in the clouds. Little had he known, this castle would one day inspire the iconic castle in Walt Disney's *Sleeping Beauty*. Ankle deep in snow, we munched on fried dough and wondered if maybe you had to be a little mad to leave behind a legacy.

Next, we drove to Innsbruck, where we took the lift up to the top of the Nordkette mountains. As we gazed down, the roads leading up the mountains looked like spilled spaghetti.

Now in Switzerland, Mom was most excited to go to Bern. Not just to experience its impressive Zytglogge, the astronomical clock in a medieval tower; the emerald river running through the city; and the faint scent of Swiss chocolate wafting through the air, but because she wanted to do family research.

My mom has always maintained that we are related to French royalty.

"We are French royalty, and when the French Revolution came' we had to get out of town and we did. We came to New Orleans." She always spoke about it so matter-of-factly after her lengthy research on ancestry.com, and I'd roll my eyes.

We entered the Gothic Bern Cathedral, the tallest cathedral in Switzerland, as a light snow fell outside. The cathedral's stone steps were so worn and smooth, they looked as if they had melted in the middle. Our breath fogged in the chilly wide-open expanse of the nave. We walked around, marveling at the stained-glass art as we searched for the names of our ancestors on the walls.

"I see it!" Mom whisper-shouted, her black glasses suspended on the bridge of her nose.

There, etched into black marble in gold letters was the name Holzer, my grandmother's maiden name. My mom did a little jig. Michael took pictures as we posed in front of the plaque, my mom and me pointing to the name.

The trip now seemed to be charged with new meaning, and I felt a spring in my step.

After a quick stop in Zurich, we were ready to move on to Paris, where I'd spend my birthday.

For my thirtieth, I had one tiny request: go to Paris and take pictures under the Eiffel Tower holding balloons with the number 30 on them. Because nothing screams "adult" like balloons. So there I stood, holding two gold balloons haplessly flailing in the wind, one with the number 3 and the other with the number 0.

"Well, I guess I won't be making Forbes 30 Under 30," I said.

Given that we were here in January, the weather in Paris was miserably cold and windy. But I just wanted one good picture, so I stripped off my coat and held the balloons by their base instead of the string, hoping to steady them enough for the camera. But it didn't work. I wanted to be a cool content creator, but I was failing.

"No, you won't make Forbes's 30 Under 30 list," my mom said, holding the coat I'd discarded to take the picture. "Were you planning on being a finalist?"

In truth, yes. I knew it was incredibly lofty, but part of me had always secretly held on to a hope that I'd do something or invent something memorable enough to warrant my name on their list.

"Oh, well," Michael said, shrugging. He put the lens cap back on the camera. "You started your own business and moved abroad—you can still be proud of your accomplishments."

But I didn't feel accomplished. And maybe I never would. Maybe life was a continuum of never feeling like you measured up. Or maybe that's just the case for most women. I've always questioned what the hell I was doing and if I was good enough. And I know for a fact that other women do too.

One time I was talking with an extraordinarily successful friend of mine, Sarah, who'd started her business from scratch with no investment at all. She now has over a dozen employees, and despite her unequivocal success, she would say, "It's not as good as it could be."

I wondered if our culture conditions women to focus on our flaws and put them out into the universe, never being quite satisfied with what we're doing.

My parents never made me feel shame about who I was or my abilities. But my mom always parented a little differently. She never told me to get up and get over it, but she also never coddled me like some mothers I knew. When I came home from school and told my mom that one of the boys had called me "thunder thighs," she didn't put it off or say, "They're just jealous and you're perfect," and then take me out for ice cream.

Instead, whenever I was upset, she would talk to me about our heritage. "You are the granddaughter of Louis Planchard the third from Louisiana. Our ancestors came from France. Marie Antoinette is your relative. Hold your head up." Now, finally, she had some proof of that.

Her words came back to me in that moment and snapped me out of my disappointment. I envisioned our ancestors being thrown out of Versailles and getting on a boat to Louisiana. If they could be ridiculed and still move forward, so could I.

In the end, Mom snapped a picture of me looking like a wet dog next to a huge dumpster instead of the Eiffel Tower with my numbered balloons. That was the picture I posted to Instagram. That was more my style, anyway.

"I guess Marie Antoinette never made the Forbes list either," I said conspiratorially to my mom as we walked down the Champs-Élysées.

"You do realize," she said, stopping on the huge boulevard to look me in the eye, "you are exactly where you're supposed to be? Maybe it's different than you imagined. Maybe your ancestors are trying to tell you something. Maybe it's the universe."

I started to roll my eyes the way only a daughter who's heard that same speech so many times can.

"Whatever it is," she began again, "you need to pay attention."

Fairy-Tale Forest

Dogs are mind readers. They know when you're about to take a trip. And they know when they're coming along. Millie and Hugo danced frantically as Michael loaded up their leashes and metal food bowls into his green backpack.

Hugo paced behind Michael's every step, constantly in the way. Then he sat reverently, as if offering good behavior for the trip.

Millie lay on the ground, her head between her front paws, and looked up at us with her almond-shaped eyes. I imagined she was trying to wordlessly bore a message into us: Take me with you. Then she sighed loudly.

"This is truly the most adorable dog I've ever seen in my life," I cooed. As if on cue, Millie rolled over and offered me her belly to scratch.

I've often been accused of using too many superlatives, most recently by the German guy in my writing group.

This is the best soup I've ever tasted!

That is the cutest sweater I've ever seen!

Maybe it's a Texas or a southern thing. Maybe it really was the cutest sweater I'd ever seen.

But now, as we headed into the legendary Black Forest, the place where nearly every fairy tale had originated, I really did feel like my use of superlatives was imperative. This was the cutest place I'd ever seen.

The Brothers Grimm get credit for the nostalgic fairy tales of our childhood, but like many tales, the stories stemmed from myths and legends, which these brothers collected over time. And the original tales are true to their name. We know the Disney versions of "Hansel and Gretel" and "Snow White," but the older versions are much more, well . . . grim.

I read one in the car as Michael drove along the winding roads, snow beginning to pile up higher and higher as we went.

"This is wild!" I said, reading "Cinderella." "It's so sinister."

"How could 'Cinderella' be sinister?" Michael asked.

"Well, it's just . . . dark. One of the evil stepsisters is cutting off her own toe, the other is cutting off her heel to fit her foot in the glass slipper. And now there's blood everywhere. Then some doves are pecking out their eyes . . ."

"Yikes," said Michael.

"Oh, this one is the darkest!" I scrolled through my phone. "This is 'The Robber Bridegroom,' so buckle up."

Michael glanced at his seat belt. "Yeah, buckled."

"Okay, this girl is going to marry the man who her father set her up with, but get this"—I read aloud—"'When they have thee in their power, they will kill thee without mercy, cook, and eat thee, for they are eaters of human flesh.'"

"So they are not only going to kill her, but also fry her up?" Michael wondered.

"Ohhh," I said, distracted by the snow, "it looks like a fairy tale!" On either side of the road, mounds of snow had now grown even taller. The evergreens that had looked at the start of our drive as if they'd been dusted with powdered sugar now drooped under the weight of the snow. They looked like something straight out of Dr. Seuss's Whoville.

"On that lovely fairy-tale note, I'm pulling over up here." Michael flicked on his turn signal and found a clearing off the road.

We got out and took in the scene, breathing in the fresh mountain air and the scent of pine. The dogs bounced in the back seat, eager to get out and explore.

We slathered Crisco on their paws to help keep the powdery snow at bay between their toes. Millie especially, with her fluffy fur, was known to get snowballs wedged in her hair. Michael glanced at his AllTrails map to find the start of the hike. The dogs easily glided up the snowbank as Michael and I grunted our way up to the trail with our hiking poles. There we were greeted with a true winter wonderland: so much snow, I couldn't tell where the horizon ended and the sky began. I envisioned Hansel and Gretel making the same trek and finding a tiny cottage.

And then, as if out of a storybook, we found our own cottage.

Nestled among the trees was a wooden barn with ornate heart-shaped lattice trim. Snow piled thickly on every exposed surface and the house's green shutters perfectly matched the surrounding pines. The dogs bounded onto the steps as if they were sure a princess was locked inside. For a flicker of a moment, I hoped we wouldn't be eaten by a witch like in the Grimm's version of the story I'd just read.

After our hike, we visited the cuckoo-clock village of Sasbachwalden, which felt like a movie set. Against the backdrop of the lush Black Forest, timbered homes and a church sat nestled like a centerpiece.

We spotted an open café called Knusperhäuschen, whose name meant "gingerbread house." A bell tinkled as we entered the warm room, the scent of coffee wafting toward us. Nearby, a fireplace crackled, illuminating a sign that read: Tradition Verpflichete erbaut im Jahre 1780. "This building has been around since 1780."

Glass displays were laden with sugared lemon tarts, glossy fruit and cheese pastries, and, of course, Black Forest cake.

"Zwei bitte," I said to the woman behind the counter, pointing to the Black Forest cake and holding up two fingers. She nodded curtly, wiped her hands on her black apron, and placed two slices on white ceramic plates.

We sat down at a wooden table covered with a red tablecloth. Two white napkins sat at our places and mismatched chairs huddled all around the room. My chair had a heart-shaped cutout and faded pink hearts on the cushion.

"There's definitely alcohol in here," I said, digging into the layers of chocolate cake, sour cherries, and whipped cream.

"Whatever it is," Michael said, swallowing a mouthful, "it's good. I can see why they make it a ritual."

The Germans' Kaffee und Kuchen, or "coffee and cake," is a midafternoon tradition similar to the British's high tea.

We were getting tired, but Michael urged us to make one last stop to see the sunset at a nearby viewpoint. I was trying to keep my eyes open but, coming down from the sugar high of the cake, I kept drifting off as we rounded the corners of the hairpin turns.

"Put on some music," Michael offered. "That will help."

As I scrolled through my Spotify playlist, I found a "Memories" playlist.

I remember driving around with my best friends during our senior year of high school and Ciara's song "Goodies" coming on the radio. Before iPods and Spotify, hearing the song you'd been waiting for was an elation like no other. Delayed gratification had made me appreciate subpar pop songs even more. But not "Goodies." To this day, that song gives me butterflies.

My friends and I were so overjoyed to hear the song that we stopped the car on the street—granted, it was a quiet neighborhood street at eleven p.m., so it was pretty much uninhabited—and leapt out and danced in the headlights. I remember looking around and, for a moment, zooming out of the scene. A fleeting feeling of sadness had draped over me: I'd never be a senior in high school again. Did that mean I'd never get to feel this way again? The finality of that realization had tugged at me.

I've always been plagued with worry that something, whatever it is, would be my last. Until I realized that seeing or doing something for the first time carries a similar weight but even more optimism. There are always new experiences to be had, and there is so much potential in the unpredictability of the future.

I decided to play "Goodies" once more on our Black Forest sunset drive. As we made our way up to the viewpoint, the sky turned cotton-candy pink. The pink was so bright, it turned the white snow a rosy sherbet; I could have scooped it into an ice cream cone.

We stepped out of the car, each holding a dog leash. The white puffs of clouds high in the sky were tinged with fuchsia as if dipped in ink. The shadows beneath the trees lengthened and stretched on either side of the lookout like lovers trying to join hands in the snow.

"Not to use a superlative, but I think this might be the best sunset I've ever seen." I smiled.

"You can definitely see how fairy tales came from here," Michael said.

I plopped down in the snow in my puffy red coat, my legs splayed out, and pulled Millie onto my lap. Michael and Hugo bounded down the hillside, Hugo flicking up snow and chasing Michael.

"Boys," I said in mock exasperation, looking down at Millie.

She agreed, glancing at them, then nuzzled her nose in the crook of my arm.

The sunset seemed to vanish suddenly, like a candle being blown out, just purple-gray smoke left behind.

"Oh, I forgot to tell you!" I said as we made our way back to the car. "Christina, Michelle, and Jordan are all pregnant. At the same time!"

"Wow, that's incredible." Michael opened the back door, and the dogs jumped in.

"I think I'm going to mail them all mini lederhosen and dirndls," I said, starting the car. These were the same girls I'd danced in the street with in high school.

"Great idea," he said.

"Michael, do you think it's weird we don't have kids?"

"Yes," he said, "but we are weird. We just watched sunset in a fairy-tale forest, ate cake in a building from the 1700s, and now we're going back to our apartment in Germany."

"Hmm," I responded thoughtfully, "yeah, that's true."

Maybe our fairy tale would have a different ending.

Butt Naked in the Baltic Sea

This wasn't the spot where you were supposed to be naked. In fact, this spot was for employees only. But there I was, standing butt naked, a constellation of red welts on my rear end, in front of thirty or so people in a Swedish sauna.

Earlier that week, we'd flown to Copenhagen, Denmark, where we rented bikes, gazed out at the rainbow buildings in Nyhavn, and experienced hygge. There isn't an exact word for hygge in English, but the main idea is coziness. But where I was standing now, I felt anything but cozy.

We'd seen that you could hop on a train and be over the Danish border into Malmö, Sweden, in just thirty minutes, so we bought tickets.

Much like in Germany, but even more so in Nordic countries, saunas are a way of life. But we hadn't been to one yet. Mostly because I am terribly self-conscious, and the idea of being naked in front of strangers gives me hives. But that wasn't the reason that I now had red spots on my butt.

The week before we visited Denmark and Sweden, we'd taken a road trip with Abdul and Letizia to go see Guns N' Roses in Hamburg and then explore Berlin.

On our drive from Heidelberg to Hamburg, I glimpsed a field of yellow canola flowers, and we pulled off the side of the road to take photos.

"There are probably tons of bugs in there," Michael warned. "You can go in, but I'm not."

He was right. I first noticed the hordes of tiny red bugs on stalks and petals, but then, to my horror, I felt them crawling up my legs and into my crotch. We had finally made some real friends, and I wasn't going to ruin it by scratching my crotch in front of them.

But my butt was so itchy, it felt like it was on fire. It was all my fault. And now it was on display. After our trip to Berlin and Hamburg, we were going to be home for less than twenty-four hours before unpacking and repacking our bags for Denmark and Sweden.

"Oh, there's a sauna in Malmö!" Michael said, looking at a pamphlet. "You jump into the Baltic Sea! I think we have to do this."

"I don't think so," I said. "Don't you get, like, completely naked?" I leaned against an ancient building in a market inside Gustaf Adolfs torg, or Gustav Adolf's square, where vendors sold flowers and vegetables.

"Yeah, but who cares? Everyone will be," Michael tried. "This is the most quintessential Swedish experience—a real bathhouse!"

"Fine. I guess I need to get over it."

"Get over it" had been my tagline for years—a phrase I'd said both to myself and to others at times when I felt particularly nervous or wary.

In the eighth grade, I had the confidence of a twenty-one-year-old on their birthday after five buttery nipple shots. Despite my slightly crooked teeth, dishwater-blonde hair, and the height of a fifth grader, I was fairly self-assured.

I was set to perform a song and dance at the St. Monica's all-schools mass to congratulate our priest for winning the NCEA award for excellence in Catholic education, an award he very much deserved. The man lived in Spain and had met Presidents Nixon and Reagan as well as Mother Teresa. The entire school, the students' parents, and even the bishop had been invited, and it was my time to shine.

I'd rehearsed after school for weeks. I'd practiced my kicks in the mirror at home. The day of the performance, I wasn't nervous—just ready to win the hearts of all those around me. I thought maybe I could get a steady gig out of it, skip high school, and move right on to performing on the Disney Channel or Nickelodeon. I'd pick up a drinking habit along the way, if necessary.

The audience hushed as the piano teacher struck the first note. We walked down the aisle of the church. Top hats cocked, we began to sing the letters N-C-E-A to the tune of "YMCA."

I looked out at the audience, a surge of adrenaline coursing through me. The kickline started, but I was in my own world. Front and center, I continued on with the song even when we'd reached the musical break. I yelled N at the complete wrong moment. The piano teacher was so thrown off that she stopped playing, and the crumpled noise of the piano ceased as wide eyes stared at me. Then I realized—I was still singing.

The moment felt like a movie I didn't want to be in.

Everyone was looking at me, silently waiting.

I had to get over it.

After a beat I stepped forward, removed my black top hat, and took a bow. I scooted back in the kickline and nodded at the piano teacher to begin again.

And now, all these years later, I was going to get over it. I'd strip naked in a Swedish sauna.

We headed down a long wooden walkway and out to the edge of a pier in the Baltic Sea, toward the pastel-green building that housed the spa. The Swedish bath Ribersborg Kallbadhus was an open-air facility with separate changing rooms for men and women. We were handed towels and instructed about the spa's different offerings: five saunas, two saltwater pools, two wood-fired hot tubs, and a sundeck. Men and women had separate baths except for one shared sauna where everyone was required to wear a towel.

"Why don't we meet at the shared sauna in about thirty minutes?" Michael suggested, and I agreed.

Inside the women's locker room, I felt sweat beading above my upper lip. Slowly, reluctantly, I peeled off my clothes, careful to hold a towel around me as I did. I watched as other women, sans towels, walked—naked and confidently—toward the various spas. Finally I, too, dropped my towel and followed.

As I headed toward a sauna, a woman about my age came up next to me, speaking Swedish.

"Oh, I'm sorry, I'm American," I answered, fighting the urge to cover myself while also trying to act as if it were totally normal to speak to someone when you were both stark naked.

"America, oooooh!" she exclaimed, opening the door. "First time here?"

"Yes." I breathed in deeply to steady myself, briefly relishing the scent of pine in the air.

"You'll love it—so relaxing and fun. But make sure to not stay too long in the sauna. Then jump in the sea after. It's—what do Americans say?—awesome!" She gave me a thumbs-up.

I sat in the hot, steamy room for as long as I could, willing myself to relax and not worry that when I got up, there would be a ring of sweat around where my naked butt cheeks had sat.

A spa attendant came in to throw water onto the glowing red rocks. Steam billowed as the temperature rose a few degrees. I couldn't take the heat anymore; it was time to go to the sea.

Even in the spring, the air was crisp, and I got chills as soon as I stepped outside. Two walkways, one for the women's side and one for the men's, ran parallel to the sea, about a half a football field apart.

It was now or never.

I ran and jumped into the water. It was ice-cold—it was wonderful! Women all around me shrieked and laughed. It didn't matter that I didn't speak Swedish—the feeling of utter insanity and jubilation took us all in.

Without a watch, I guessed that it was about time to meet Michael at the joint sauna. Feeling much more confident now, I strolled back toward the saunas, getting lost in the maze of white and pastel buildings. I'm sure there was a sign that read "Do not enter," but it would have been in Swedish. Besides, I thought I knew where I was going.

. . . Until I saw an employee, fully clothed in white, waving at me. It was clear I wasn't supposed to be there. I turned around in slow motion and, to my utter horror, realized I was standing in front of the shared sauna. Red butt cheeks and all.

"I'm sorry, but I was laughing," Michael said, still giggling. I'd finally found my way back to the women's locker room, grabbed my towel, and made it back to the joint sauna.

I started laughing too. I knew I should have felt more embarrassed, but I didn't. Maybe it was the lingering thrill from jumping into the icy Baltic Sea. Maybe it was that I had realized that being naked certainly wasn't that big of a deal. Maybe I really did "get over it"—life was too short not to go skinny-dipping in the Baltic Sea, even if it meant that you might find yourself standing naked in the employees-only area of a bathhouse in front of fifty towel-clad Swedes.

Graveyard Toilets

We were definitely heading in the wrong direction on a narrow one-way street outside of Monaco. The winding roads were an unending maze. If I thought driving in Italian cities like Milan and Lake Como was hard, this countryside was like the Wild West—no rules.

"Turn left!" I hollered.

"Where? Here?" Michael asked.

"Um, back there. We missed it."

"It's okay," he said, sighing. Then grimacing.

It was not okay. We were lost and we were already on each other's last nerve.

A few weeks ago, we'd made the decision to try working together, but it wasn't really our ideal scenario—for a number of reasons. After Michael's parents had tried working together, they'd gotten a divorce. And we'd heard so many horror stories about relationships crumbling after husbands and wives mixed business with their personal lives. Plus, the blog was called "Helene in Between." I'd started it and grown it, and I didn't want Michael to feel like an outsider.

But Michael hated his job and was barely making any money, and the person I'd recently hired to help me with the blog and social media was proving to not be very helpful. I didn't want to go through the hiring process again, and I knew that Michael had the skills. He was extremely detail-oriented. Recently he'd made an Excel spreadsheet to determine which duvet cover out of dozens we should buy. He'd even written a formula calculating the price per gram for each. When he finally selected one, despite having teased him, I couldn't deny that we had the best duvet I'd ever slept with.

So, I knew Michael could rock it. I just had no idea how to delegate. I was so used to doing everything and felt silly asking him to respond to emails when I knew I could just do it myself.

But the plan was to try it . . . and see how it went. Either of us could say, "This isn't working" at any time, and that would be the end of our collaboration. Our relationship came first—both of us prioritized that—but we still didn't know how to navigate it in the context of being colleagues. So far, we were bickering more and more. I was afraid that resentment was creeping in.

To add further stress, our visas had been denied yet again. But with our lawyer's support, my new business plan, and some additional paperwork, this time we were more organized and had a strategy in place. We resubmitted our application.

And it was denied a third time.

The German immigration office in Heidelberg requested that we provide more income statements.

We decided to meet with our lawyer in person to make sure we had everything in order before submitting our visa application again. I drummed my fingers and gnawed on my nails in her tepid office as we took turns shuffling through the paperwork. In the distance, I heard the jarring sound of a siren—wailing a different tune than we were used to hearing—and it felt like an ominous warning, signaling our final shot to stay in Germany.

Our lawyer was older, her gray hair coiffed on top of her head in a black clip. Her thick glasses hung at the end of her nose. She made no small talk, gave no pleasantries, just slid our paperwork across the slick mahogany tabletop.

"There," she said, tapping the documents. "That should do it. I believe you will now get approval. I feel good about this."

I smiled. "Okay."

But Michael sat frozen, looking down at the paperwork.

"Everything is all sent in, and you should hear back shortly," our lawyer went on. "It could be two days. It could be two weeks. I am not sure. But we will see." She crossed her arms and sat back in her chair, as if to indicate that the meeting was over.

She left the room, and Michael's face grew pale. He pointed to the top of the cover page. My blog name was written incorrectly. Instead of heleneinbetween.com, it was helene-in-between.com. As we flipped through the document, we realized in horror that the misspelling was at the top right-hand corner of every single page. All twenty-six pages.

This was the part of the paperwork that had already been submitted. I thought I was going to throw up, right then and there. I envisioned the German immigration officers looking up my website and laughing: She tried to pull a fast one on us—her website's not even real! Then I imagined them barging into our apartment and throwing us out.

Once, in middle school, I forgot to turn in a signed permission slip for a field trip. As the teacher came by, I quickly forged my mom's signature.

"Is this really your mom's signature?" the teacher had asked, scanning my messy scrawl.

"Um . . . yes?" I responded as a question.

"So I could call your mom and she would say she signed this?"

"No," I broke, my bottom lip quivering.

"Detention. For forging a signature and for lying, Helene," my teacher scolded.

I'd never had detention before. That was for future criminals! Outcasts! It would be a scandal. I wanted to throw up.

And that was exactly how I felt looking down at the paper now, but times a thousand. I definitely wasn't in middle school anymore.

Holding back tears, I considered our options. How could I salvage this situation as quickly as possible? It was too late to submit new paperwork with the correct website address. I navigated to GoDaddy on my phone and searched for "helene-in-between," holding my breath. It was available! And for $9.99, it could be all mine. I bought the new domain name and rerouted it to heleneinbetween.com.

Michael and I both tried the website—it worked.

Now we'd just have to wait some more on the outcome of our visa.

"Let's pull over," Michael said, pointing to a clearing perched above the city of Monaco.

As we rounded into a gravel driveway, I saw that we'd come upon a cemetery. A cemetery with a fabulous seaside view of one of the most lavish and expensive cities in the world, Monaco, a sovereign city-state stretching just a mile long near the French Riviera.

We walked among the old gravestones and out toward the edge of the cemetery, frustration and uncertainty about our visas rendering us silent.

"I'm going to the bathroom," I said, breaking the silence, then climbed up a few stone steps to a small outdoor restroom. It had a toilet, yellowed with age and lined with calcified water rings indicating old water levels. Wet toilet paper littered the ground, and the smell was terrible enough to make the people buried outside turn in their graves.

After I peed, I pulled up my shorts and then—clunk. I whipped around to see that I'd dropped my phone into the decrepit toilet bowl. My new iPhone was supposedly waterproof . . . or so I hoped. I guess we'll see, I thought. I shoved my hand into the yellow-gray bowl, yanked out my phone, and ran outside, stripping off the protective case.

"I just dropped my phone in the damn toilet!" I screeched.

"Turn it off!" Michael urged.

I wiped my phone off with a dirty T-shirt from my backpack and set it on the car hood to dry while we snapped a few more pictures and walked around. Despite the frantic mishap, the stunning beauty of the place wasn't completely lost on me. I took it all in: crystal-clear blue waves frothed and foamed; yachts bobbed near the dock; elegant men and women in perfectly tailored suits and dresses strolled beneath us; shiny, slick Rolls-Royces cruised the streets; high-end shops stretched along the promenade, crowned with the Casino de Monte-Carlo, which looked like a palace.

And there were Michael and I in our shorts and T-shirts, my toilet-water-soaked hand held off to the side, as far as possible from the rest of my body. We were still brimming with anger after the meeting with the lawyer.

"Oh no," I said, looking up at Michael. "My phone had the confirmation and directions for the hotel tonight."

He squinted at me. "I'm sure it will turn back on."

It didn't.

After gawking at the intricate marble in Monaco and laughing at the outrageous prices of a Coca-Cola Light (we couldn't find any Diet Coke in Europe), we used Michael's phone to navigate our way to our next stop, the hilltop town of Èze, France.

In Èze, I imagined myself as Belle from *Beauty and the Beast*, traipsing down stone steps and singing "Bonjour" to passersby. Sitting atop a hill, Èze is a well-preserved medieval town completely encased in stone. Everyone is friendly—even cats seem to say hello when you walk by. Tiny perfume shops line the streets, so the entire town smells like fresh lavender.

We should be happy, I thought, gazing through the purple haze at the view of the Côte d'Azur, rocky cliffs dotted with white stone houses and orange tile roofs stacked like steps toward the edge of the Mediterranean.

Michael spoke at length to a man who had just come back from truffle hunting with his dog in the surrounding forest. Then we stopped at Château Eza and drank wine and watched the sun set.

Now we were trying to find our hotel in Nice in the dark.

"I'm pretty sure I said left," I told Michael, my phone still refusing to turn on. Luckily, he had found the hotel reservation on his phone.

"No, you didn't," he said curtly. "You absolutely said right."

I probably did say right when it was a left. We were tired, I'd had too much wine, and it was dark. If I thought Italy was difficult to drive in, stone-lined roads in France were proving perhaps more challenging.

"Okay, right!" I shouted. "Wait, I mean left!"

"Jesus, Helene, are you serious?"

"It's there! I see it!" The lighted sign emblazoned with Hôtel was like a beacon in the sea of night.

After finding a tiny spot to parallel park, we wearily put on our backpacks and headed to the check-in desk.

"No," the woman at the check-in desk said. "No tonight."

She spoke broken English, and we spoke broken French, desperately trying to use Google Translate to explain that we'd booked a room for tonight.

"No!" she said, throwing up her hands. "Tomorrow."

I looked down at the reservation.

"Michael," I said, "you booked the hotel for tomorrow night."

Deflated, we headed back to the car to look for a hotel last minute. We found one, twenty minutes away.

We stared in silence as we drove, watching the white traffic stripes slip by.

"There are no billboards in France!" I said, glancing around the freeway, attempting to cut the tension.

France was trying to get rid of billboards. In Texas, like many US states, billboards were plentiful along the highways, eager for attention. In Dallas, there's an iconic billboard for a lawyer named Jim Adler, aka "the Texas Hammer." I always knew I was close to home when I started seeing his billboards.

Michael didn't reply.

I looked up and saw a castle in the distance. Maybe the French knew they were home when they started to see familiar castles.

I tried to think of what signified the same feeling now of being "home," but nothing resonated. Heidelberg still didn't feel like that.

And maybe it never would.

A Mountain Girl

Now that we had hiking poles, I felt we'd finally begun to assimilate into German culture. But we still didn't have visas, and if we didn't secure them soon, we'd no longer be allowed to live here.

We were still working on that.

But even with my hiking poles, I didn't have the German look down. Were they all fit? It seemed so. Despite eating unlimited pretzels, beer, schnitzel, and gelato. When it's one euro a scoop, how do you not order two?

Despite all the good food, I had gotten fitter. But not German fit.

On Sundays, since most establishments were closed, Germans often took to the outdoors and went hiking or biking, or they lounged like lizards in the sun. Germans flocked outside during sunny days, even taking time off from work. And they had so many vacation days, that was easy to do. Most Germans are required to get twenty days off, not including holidays. I thought about my five vacation days at my old nine-to-five and opened my laptop to write a blog post. I couldn't imagine going back to a cubicle in an overly air-conditioned office.

If we were at home, in Heidelberg, we'd head to the nearby hills with the dogs and climb up and up, past the outdoor kindergarten and into the woods.

But now it was time to put our hiking skills to the test in Austria.

The most hiking I'd ever done was an expert-level route in the Grand Canyon, which was not recommended during the hot summer months. Michael and I went with friends, and Josh and Michael picked out the hike, checking with the group. Unfortunately, the rest of us waved them off: "Sure, sure, whatever you guys want to do." It was summer, and we were not experts. The hike started downhill, toward the canyon, before an uphill battle on the return.

It will be easier on the way back, I thought.

I was wrong.

My weak ankle began to shake on our way back up the rocky trail, where one slip could have meant death.

We'd made it out alive. But I wasn't going to take my chances in Austria.

As we headed toward the Alps, the razor-sharp peaks jutted out like teeth, grazing the bright blue sky. The mountains were draped with a blanket of snow, and I could make out white crosses mounted on some of the taller peaks. Below were rolling hills dotted with gleaming white steepled churches. The balconies of weathered bed-and-breakfast pensions held boxes overflowing with red and pink flowers.

We rolled down the windows and threaded our fingers through the wind, breathing in the fresh mountain air as we listened to the

Chicks' (then called The Dixie Chicks) "Wide Open Spaces," singing until our voices cracked.

Maybe I liked the mountains after all? I'd always considered myself to be a beach girl. My family wasn't a mountain family; we were a beach family. We didn't do après-ski. We went crabbing. Every summer, we'd load up into the minivan: my mom and dad, my sisters, and I, along with ice chests, neon plastic sand toys, and deflated inner tubes. We'd drive fourteen hours from Dallas, Texas, to Seaside, Florida, a truly idyllic slice of Americana—it was where *The Truman Show* had been filmed.

Rows of multicolored pastel houses with white trim lined the black top streets that led up to wood walkways that stretched out to sugar-sand beaches. The highway, 30A, snaked along the coast, where beaches were dappled with towns like Seaside, Watercolor, or Grayton, each offering tourists an escape from city life—beach chairs with umbrellas and frozen daiquiris.

My mom had started going to Destin, Florida, as a child and brought me before I could walk. But as the high-rises got higher, she made her way down the coastline until she found 30A. We'd walk the beach, hunt for shells and sand dollars, and watch sunsets. Toward the end of our one-week trips, we'd go crabbing.

My parents would load up the crab nets with raw chicken and we'd head out to Destin's bay, where my sisters and I would take turns roping in the crabs, screaming with delight every time we caught one. Then we'd take them back to the condo for Mom to boil them up. We'd melt butter and have fresh crab for days, my sand-dusted feet dangling off my chair as I dipped crab meat into melted butter.

I always thought I preferred the beach—until I went to Wilder Kaiser, Austria. Much like Highway 30A, the Wilder Kaiser area comprises idyllic villages, each one slightly different from the last. Festivals and hiking are popular in the warmer months, and snow sports in the cold.

When we pulled into our hotel, Au Pension, in the town of Söll, a jolly pink-cheeked man in his mid-thirties greeted us and our dogs. It had been a surprise and a comfort to discover how easy it was to find dog-friendly places nearly everywhere.

"Willkommen to Au Pension!" he said, shaking our hands and patting each dog on the head.

He showed us to our room: a simple wood-paneled suite that smelled of pine. Pristine white linens covered the bed, and the back door opened onto a patio that looked out to the jagged mountains.

"Breakfast is included," the man said, then handed us our key attached to a large plastic yellow disc.

Breakfast was not your typical toast and eggs. Of course, there were eggs, but there were also four different kinds of breads, seven different homemade spreads, various sliced meats, yogurt, and milks. Michael was thrilled with the different milk offerings.

I spooned a thick golden syrup onto my toast, thinking it was honey but it was like no honey I'd ever tasted; it was like liquid gold.

"What is this?" I asked the pink-cheeked man.

"This"—he said, holding the jar to the light, as if presenting the crown jewels—"is forest honey."

"Oh, so it is honey!" I exclaimed.

"No!" he bellowed. "Not at all. No bees. We clip the new growth off the evergreen trees, boil it down for three days, add sugar, and boil it more."

"It's one of the best things I've ever tasted in my life," I said.

Michael and I bought a jar. I've bought cheap souvenirs before, and they usually get tossed in a drawer where they're quickly forgotten. Instead, local delicacies were quickly becoming our favorite way to bring back memories of the smells and tastes from our trips.

More than culinary discoveries, we were embarking on something entirely brand-new to Michael: skiing. I was by no means an expert myself—I'd only been skiing once. I could rope in a crab, no problem. Build a sandcastle? You got it. But mountains? They just weren't my thing.

The one time I'd gone skiing was with Life Teen, a religious group for teens that organized extracurriculars after church. I grew up Catholic, I went to Catholic schools, and I attended church every Sunday. But I wasn't particularly religious. I did it to spend time with boys.

For Life Teen, we drove twelve hours on a bus from Dallas, Texas, to Breckenridge, Colorado. A few teens got caught attempting to create a life in the bathroom bus. I barely skied on that trip, mostly because I was more interested in the hot tub and making out. Also, after Christina broke her wrist, and Josh (yes, the same one) broke his leg, I steered clear of the slopes.

But here I was, attempting to ski again. There was only one problem: the ski instructor. Our guide was a little too handsome in a way that I wasn't sure if I could trust him. Maybe he got the job because of his jawline?

Now was not the time to fall and injure my leg again. I was just starting to feel like I could do jumping jacks without pain after my rock-climbing fall. But now I was staring down the bunny hill as if it were Everest.

I zipped my red coat up to my chin and adjusted my sunglasses. I hadn't bothered to get goggles—they were twelve euros and I didn't think I'd need them.

"So do we do pizza all the way down?" Michael asked, pointing the toes of his skis together to mimic the shape of a pizza slice. "Is that the move?"

"That's a good start," the instructor said, flashing his perfectly white teeth. "But the best idea is to flex your ankles and stay limber, with your skis parallel as you balance slowly down."

Flex my ankle? With eight screws and a metal plate, there wasn't a whole lot of room for flexing.

We listened to our instructor for the first turn on the bunny hill, then pizza'ed the rest of the way.

"Oh yes, you are American. You love your pizza!" he said, laughing.

I'd found Austrians to be direct and to-the-point like Germans but in a kinder, more fun way. By the end of our lesson, Michael and I were still terrible, but we were a little bit more confident. As we clomped our way back to the ski rental shop, we saw some people sledding.

"Now that looks fun," Michael said.

We rented beautiful wooden sleds complete with metal runners and a rope. I had gone "sledding" in Dallas when it snowed once every other year. We'd drag our laundry baskets up and slide down for about five seconds.

But this was different. The rope on this sled—a toboggan—wasn't even necessary. We took the lift up, higher and higher. Austria had dedicated sledding runs.

We spent hours going up the lift and down on the sled, Michael going so fast that the snow he kicked up caked his mustache and beard.

"My face hurts so much!" he said gleefully. "That was amazing!"

On our last day, we brought the dogs on a shorter run to see if they could gallop along. I looked out to the white peaks of the snowy Alps and breathed in. The air smelled like the Bath & Body Works "Fresh Balsam," except it was the real thing.

People told me I'd never know real love until I had a child, but had they ever stood on top of a mountain with a dog, fresh bread, and a jar of forest honey? That could be true love too. Maybe I was a mountain girl after all.

Two O'Clock at Trevi

It was too hot. I'm from Texas, so I'm used to the heat. But this kind of heat is inescapable.

There's very little air-conditioning on the continent of Europe. In some places like Norway or Ireland, it doesn't really matter. But in Rome in the summer, it does—especially as tourists pile into the Colosseum, pound the cobblestone streets to the Pantheon, and pour into the Vatican.

Italy is shocking in its ancient beauty. I thought nothing could top the magnitude of the Milan Cathedral or the serene beauty of Lake Como. But I was wrong. In the floating city of Venice, adorned with winding canals and marble palaces, we got lost in the maze of water and ate two gelatos a day. Then, in Florence, we watched the sun set along the Ponte Vecchio and climbed the 463 steps to the top of Florence's Duomo.

And now, in Rome, strolling along on the cobblestone streets, I felt a momentous energy, as if each step I took landed in a spot of historical significance. The city of Rome has had trouble building new structures because every time they excavate a spot to build, they uncover some ancient relic. In fact, just recently, a metro expansion came to an abrupt halt after workers found an entire dwelling from the second century.

More than any other place, Rome holds a mythical quality for me. My dad studied abroad there for nine months, then traveled throughout Europe and other parts of the world. He even ventured to places like Afghanistan. Before this, the only place he'd traveled to outside of his home state of Louisiana was to Ohio to sell Bibles. He came back from Europe a full-fledged hippie.

That trip left a lasting impression on my dad that he still savors today. Would it have the same effect on me? I hoped so. Not that I wanted to start wearing bell bottoms and flowers in my hair. I just wanted to feel different.

I glanced out from the Roman Forum, which stretched between the Palatine and Capitoline Hill, standing sentry. I tried to imagine the ruins in their heyday, Emperor Titus himself in a horse-drawn chariot, heading into the Colosseum to watch the gladiators fight to the death. But death, apparently, was much rarer than Hollywood movies would have us believe.

We had a lot to learn.

Michael and I knew we'd never see all of Europe in three years. In our lifetime. In a century! After popping into a dozen or so Roman churches, each one more glorious than the last, it was clear: there was no way to see it all. It was also clear why many Europeans had shifted to become nonpracticing Christians. The churches were like palaces: opulent and ornate, overflowing with gold mosaics, delicate stained-glass windows that told stories from the Bible, and intricate carvings done by Michelangelo, Caravaggio, and Bernini. I could imagine that if I were starving in the streets, I'd be frustrated with the sheer wealth of the church.

But here we were, exhausted from the overwhelming glory that was Italy, just a fifty-euro, two-hour plane ride away.

Our feet were weary from walking twenty thousand steps before noon—we needed a rest. We found a café near the Spanish Steps, and I had to have this bright orange drink everyone seemed to be sipping.

It was an Aperol spritz, and it was very expensive. Michael ordered a limoncello. The ice in my Aperol spritz didn't help much to ease the heat, but I put my wrists against the condensation on the glass and willed my body to cool down. The café in the middle of the street was shaded by large tan awnings, their flaps barely lifting in the occasional oven-hot breeze. Two-top tables covered in plastic tablecloths printed with lemons were secured by metal clips so they didn't blow away.

"Will you take a photo of me with my drink?" I asked.

Michael lifted our hand-me-down Nikon camera, which my sister had discarded after a high school photography class. We were still getting the hang of who should do what when it came to our online business, but it was clear that Michael should take the photos. A week ago he snapped one of St. Mark's Square in Venice just as the sun was setting, casting a pink haze across the golden buildings. I was convinced he should submit it to *Condé Nast*.

"Lens cap," I reminded him.

"Oh yeah," he said, snapping exactly one photo. "You want more?" He peered behind the camera.

"Yes. I don't know. Take a few, I guess." I adjusted my cat-eye sunglasses.

"Then do something different."

I always feel awkward posing for photos, unsure what to do with my hands—or my face, for that matter. But I was convinced that the more pictures we took, the more likely there would be one worth posting on Instagram.

"Okay, okay, that's enough," I said hurriedly, my cheeks turning red. I had just seen a tourist order a cappuccino, much to the dismay of our waiter, who was now on his way over to us with our bill. I didn't want to be taking photos for Instagram when he approached us.

If Germans have rules about everything, Italians have rules about food: no cappuccino after eleven a.m., no alfredo sauce ever, pasta isn't the main course, pizza is not precut, and dinner isn't until eight p.m. at the earliest. While some of these rules baffled me, I also loved how passionate Italians were about food and drink. It was an art.

And clearly, they were serious about art, too.

Earlier that day, we'd toured the Vatican, where Michael had a beer on top of St. Peter's Basilica. Standing at the top of the Sistine Chapel, whose paintings are some of the world's most famous and most cherished, while having an alcoholic beverage isn't frowned upon. In fact, a nun was the one who'd handed him the beer. But order a latte later in the day, and you're the weird one.

A few days earlier in Florence, we ate a breakfast pastry while walking past the Duomo, up the street toward the Uffizi Gallery for a tour, and people looked at us like we were insane. Eating and walking is simply not done. I imagined Italians dressed in their crisp blue polos, designer jeans, and inexplicably clean tennis shoes taking one look at us and instantly knowing we were Americans.

"They are always rushing," they'd joke.

Despite the move abroad, Michael and I hadn't yet slowed down. The more we saw, the more we wanted to see. When my sisters and I were growing up, my mom would always have us write lists in a spiral notebook she kept. I'd made lists of things I wanted to accomplish. Michael liked making lists of goals too. Because how else would you remember what you wanted to achieve?

My goals had started out broad: travel, write a book, have

my own business. Now, after visiting more and more places, I was setting new, more specific goals—making plans and writing down what I wanted out of life. The thought that Michael and I couldn't do it all wasn't sad; it was motivating. There was so much beauty in the world, and I was mesmerized by it all.

We continued to make our way through the busy streets toward the Trevi Fountain, passing more cafés and expensive Aperol spritzes. When we reached the fountain, our mouths hung open at the scene in front of us. The large open semicircle around the fountain, as well as the steps leading down toward it, were absolutely crawling with people. Tourists buckled up to the sides of the walls, it was so densely packed. I made sure my black Fossil crossbody bag was zipped and followed Michael through the throngs of people.

The Trevi Fountain is nearly one hundred feet tall and sits under an arch. It's filled with gleaming white statues; at its center stands the menacing stone carving of Neptune, god of the sea.

"Is everyone in the world in Rome or is it just me?" I asked Michael, shouting over the hum of the crowd.

"This is wild. It's so busy!" Michael answered. "I don't think I've ever seen any place so crowded. It's going to be hard to get a picture of you without anyone in it."

"I think I'm past that point," I said. "I just want to throw a coin in and get out of here." I unzipped my bag and dug around to look for two pennies. I handed one to Michael just as a woman taking a selfie bumped into me, sending my wallet, our hotel room key, and my lipsticks onto the ground.

I wiped sweat from my forehead and sighed, picking everything back up. Michael threw his coin in and made a wish—all Trevi wishes are the same: that you'll return to Rome one day. I picked up my coin, and Michael lifted the camera, ready to take a photo. Just before raising up my right hand to throw the shiny penny over my shoulder, I glanced down at my watch.

It was two p.m. It was two p.m. on a Tuesday and I was in Rome, about to throw a coin into Trevi Fountain. I wasn't at my desk at work in a cubicle. I wasn't even on one of my once- or twice-a-year trips.

This was my life now.

"Wait!" I screamed.

"What?" Michael said, lowering the camera.

"I just looked at my watch. It's two p.m. on a Tuesday. And look where we are."

Michael looked at me and smiled, then pulled me in for a hug. "We did it. We're here, together."

The moment seemed frozen in time, as if I were stepping outside of myself, suspended from above as I looked down at the chaotic, beautiful scene: tourists and thousand-year-old architecture. I was working for myself, with my husband, and traveling the world.

It was two p.m. on a Tuesday, and this was my life.

The Verdict

I am not *not* superstitious. If I see a penny, you're dang right I'm going to pick it up so all day long I have good luck. I'm not going to walk under an open ladder, but that just seems like good common sense. And sure, I'd knock on wood to ensure that we would be awarded our visas.

But I would absolutely step on cracks without fear of breaking my mother's back. I wasn't that nuts.

At this point, I didn't have any more nails to bite; they were quite literally bitten down to the quick, which is both painful and unattractive. But I couldn't contain my nerves. Would we get to legally live in Germany?

After so much back-and-forth, denials and lawyers, business plans and meetings, we were expecting a final decision any day now. So, for the time being, Michael and I attempted to live life as normally as we possibly could—which also meant following the German superstition we'd learned at Oktoberfest: make eye contact when clinking glasses to avoid bad luck (and bad sex) for seven years.

And what was normal now anyway? Normal was spending a week in Bulgaria, two weeks driving on the left side of the road on the coast of Ireland, and biking to the neighboring town of Schwetzingen with friends.

I'd stopped letting work and our looming visa situation hinder me from living my life, and we were doing what we'd moved abroad for in the first place: traveling. Really traveling. We made a bucket list of places to visit in Europe—and of course Michael made an Excel spreadsheet.

The past few weeks had been a testament to our endeavor.

Bulgaria hadn't been on that initial list, but I scribbled it in and then crossed it out after our trip. When we found a cheap flight and the Best Western in Sofia, Bulgaria offered us a free stay, we jumped at the chance. The city was incredible, and everyone we interacted with was so kind. The cabdriver even brought our camera back to our hotel after Michael left it in the back seat. Anywhere else, it would have been long gone.

"You, uh . . ." the cabdriver spoke with exaggerated warmth, holding the camera like a precious antique. "You left in my cab."

Sofia, the country's capital, was a mix of architectural styles: grand cathedrals, blocky Soviet-era buildings, and modern cafés alongside ancient Roman ruins. It reminded me a bit of the much more popular Vienna, Austria, minus the tourists. An actual yellow-brick road ran through town, a gift from Austria's emperor Franz Joseph.

Outside the city, we ventured to the natural wonder of Seven Rila Lakes, where we trekked through lush alpine meadows to mirrorlike glacial lakes that perfectly reflected the surrounding mountains.

But my favorite spot? The Rila Monastery. Tucked in the mountains, the monastery looked more like a fortress with its high stone walls and tall towers. Inside was a complex of intricately decorated striped buildings reminiscent of Tuscan architecture, with colorful frescoes and elaborate wood carvings. We stayed until the museum closed, exploring the treasure trove of Bulgaria's history.

I'd finally figured out that I could travel and blog at the same time. Things wouldn't fall apart.

On our trip to Ireland, we met up with Josh and his wife, Kelly, at the tail end of their honeymoon. We planned to spend the whole week in Dublin and take day trips from there, but after Josh had managed to drive on the "wrong" side of the road, Michael felt he had to try too.

We made our way into the neon-green Irish countryside, winding through narrow streets with three-foot-high stone fences on one side and sheer cliffs on the other. We ate Irish soda bread with cheese and stopped at the quintessential Kilkenny Castle, kissed the Blarney Stone for the gift of eloquence (and I threw in finally getting our visas for good measure), and watched dogs herd sheep at Killarney National Park. Then we watched the birds at the Cliffs of Moher, mesmerized by how they managed to withstand the brutal gales.

Spring in Germany was the loveliest season of all, we soon found out. Roses in every shade imaginable, some the size of your head, crept up and poked out of garden fences as if begging to be seen. The soft morning light filtered through pink cherry blossom trees swaying in the breeze, weighed down with so many flowers that we couldn't even see their branches. My walks up Philosophenweg were getting easier; my muscles had gotten stronger from walking and biking everywhere.

We biked with Abdul and Letizia from Heidelberg to Schwetzingen, where we found statues dedicated to asparagus, or Spargel. The entire country went wild for Spargel season, and the Germans put green and "golden" white asparagus on everything: pizza, pasta, soup—I wouldn't have been surprised to find asparagus ice cream.

"We'll never run out of places to explore," Michael said as we biked back to Heidelberg, and I couldn't help but agree.

Next up, Michael and I began a three-week road trip through Romania, then down Croatia's Dalmatian coast, and ending with a cruise through Norway's fjords.

Most days I woke up before my alarm clock buzzed, my eyes shooting open. I would pull my phone up by the power cord, tug our blue duvet over my head, and check my email.

One morning I immediately noticed a message from our lawyer, sent just minutes earlier. The subject line read simply: The decision of the immigration office for your information below.

Before scrolling any further, I lightly tapped Michael on the shoulder and he instantly woke up. He was an extraordinarily light sleeper, and he always felt the opposite of how I felt in the morning: not quite ready for the world. He'd shuffle his feet as not to have to pick them up while barely opening his eyes, like a teenager dreading going to school in the morning.

He looked at me through the slits of his eyelids, his hair ruffled, and waited for me to speak.

"We have the news on our visa. I wanted to wait to read it with you," I said, trying to temper my voice.

Together, we headed downstairs, the dogs at our heels. Michael had trained them not to walk past us down the stairs so we wouldn't trip. I'd never been more thankful for that than right then; my nerves threatened to lock my knees.

Michael settled into his black rolling office chair while I pulled up one of the wooden ones from our dining room table. We had inherited the lovely wooden table and two chairs from the previous owner, who had used them as patio furniture. We had repurposed them for our dining room.

"Okay." Michael let out a long exhale as he opened the email and clicked on the blue "Translate to English" button so we could properly decipher the verdict.

"'Ladies and gentleman,'" I read, and my mind spun to images of a circus show.

Helene, focus!

"'Mr. and Mrs. Sula can now be granted a residence permit for one year.'"

We have visas!

We could officially live in Germany. It had taken us eight months and a lawyer, but finally our stay had been approved. Not unsurprisingly, Germany was still keeping us on our toes: they hadn't granted the full three years we'd requested, but one was better than nothing. We'd have another appointment with the immigration office to get all the necessary paperwork for the final visas. The appointment wasn't until May 29, but I didn't care. We finally had approval.

This was it—the final step in our journey to move abroad. It solidified our ability to realize the dream we'd been chasing since that first magical trip back in 2012. Well, knock on wood.

We went out for celebratory drinks at the nearby River Café and toasted—while looking into each other's eyes, of course. We didn't want to risk bad luck.

"Wow, this was a freaking long time coming," Michael said, taking a gulp of the German Riesling.

"I still can't believe it took this long, but we did it." I set down my glass on the crisp white tablecloth. Despite being called River Café, the restaurant had no view of the river, just a street lined with red-roofed white stucco shops.

A single white taper candle stood at the center of our table, and we sat silently, staring at the flame.

"Hey," I said, snapping us out of our reverie, "when we get home, let's remember to gr—"

"Whoa," Michael said, putting his hand on my arm.

"What?" I asked, confused.

"You just said 'home.' 'When we get home . . .' You've never called it home before." His lips curved into a grin.

"You know what? You're right . . . This is home."

And I drained the rest of my wine.

You Can Sleep When
You're Dead

The day felt like someone had punched a hole in the clouds. I was flooded with incandescent warmth as I got off the train from Heidelberg to Paris. The early morning light bounced theatrically against the backdrop of the Parisian boulevards.

It's hard to *not* feel like you're in a movie in Paris. Exquisite white stone carvings popped against black wrought-iron balconies that lined the streets, and in the distance stood the Sacré-Couer, imposing, peeking behind every corner. The apartments seemed to lean into each other, whispering secrets.

Most likely gossiping about my outfit—a very unfashionable dress and tennis shoes. I hadn't mastered "French girl chic" yet, and I probably never would.

And then I stepped in dog poop.

No matter. I was in Paris! Alone in Paris, on my first ever solo trip. And I was getting paid to be here. Not even dog poop could dampen my spirit.

I scuffed the bottoms of my white Reeboks on the curb and continued on toward the Palais Garnier, the opera house.

Traveling alone felt different. With my red backpack pressed tightly against my shoulders and my camera slung around my neck—lens cap off, ready to snap a photo—I buzzed with energy. The city seemed to gleam around me.

I considered what had brought me here: for the first time, a travel company had hired me to share about my experiences abroad. This was my first ever paid trip (in Paris, of all places!). I was determined to prove I was worth the company's resources. I envisioned other companies seeing my work and hiring me to go to their destinations.

Once in my room—a loft with slanted ceilings and purple velvet furnishings—I checked my schedule. I had a loose list of activities I needed to do on my three-day trip. One, I was thrilled to see, was a guided culinary tour of Montmartre. I'd spend a few days traveling around the city, and then I'd share a blog post and Instagram stories detailing my experiences.

I stopped and looked around my room, my eyes landing on a chilled bottle of champagne with a note: Welcome to Paris, Helene in Between!

I grinned to myself, relishing the moment.

Since the tour wasn't until dinner, I spent the whole day walking around the city, looking at it through a new, independent lens.

I gazed up at the gargoyles that peered down from the spiny roofline of the Notre-Dame. I strolled along the embankments of the Seine River, watching the sellers, the Bouquinistes of Paris, organize their secondhand and antique books in their green box stalls. I crossed the Pont Neuf bridge and headed to Sainte-Chapelle, my favorite chapel in the world, with its floor-to-ceiling intricate stained glass. I stood stationary in the middle of the marble floor, transfixed by the chapel's beauty, as tourists flowed all around me. Outside, purple wisteria drooped from cafés and cherry blossoms fluttered in the breeze. I imagined Ernest Hemingway furiously scribbling away a masterpiece in a café. I had to agree with him: Paris was a movable feast.

Yes, I had been to Paris before. But my familiar twinge of nostalgia was noticeably absent; gone was my fixation on memories, my obsession with living in the past. The world unfolded around me: for once, I was present and fully immersed.

For so long, I'd let nostalgia guide my life. I looked back on the past with such reverence that I often failed to embrace the beauty of the present. In German, they call this feeling Sehnsucht, a word that translates to "longing," "desire," or "yearning." Some psychologists use it to describe thoughts and emotions related to the unfinished or imperfect aspects of life, coupled with an ache for idealized alternative experiences. I always wanted to capture and relive past feelings of elation, so much so that too often I'd missed out on joy in the present.

It took traveling the world to shift my perspective. I learned that new adventures held tremendous value and that exploring new places could rekindle the initial enchantment I felt when I was younger. That nostalgia would never go away, of course; it's part of me, and it's made me who I am. But I no longer let it rule my life or make me feel sad or distant in the present. I now appreciate my past but relish the present and regard the future with hope.

I realized, with a jolt—stopping suddenly in the middle of a cobblestone street as a thought hit me—I don't have to travel to truly live. A fulfilling life could take many forms, and it was about choosing to embrace opportunity, to take risks . . . even when it was scary.

My stomach growled. I grabbed a croissant and a Coca-Cola Light and made my way to the meeting point for the tour—a windmill, Moulin de la Galette, once used to grind flour and press grapes in the 1700s. It inspired the art community that flourished in Montmartre in the 1800s. Renoir, Van Gogh, Toulouse-Lautrec, Picasso had all lived here. Now the Moulin de la Galette was a meeting spot for tourists.

Our guide was a rambunctious older gentleman who looked more like a retired boxer than a tour guide, with deep grooves in his face that drew his mouth into a half frown. The group of a dozen or so of us formed a semicircle around him as he folded his arms over his starched blue button-down and waited patiently.

Then he gracefully lifted his hand and pointed to the windmill. "Welcome to the most important arrondissement of Paris: Montmartre," he said in heavily accented English.

We followed closely behind our guide as he detailed Montmartre's rich history: Roman temples from the seventh century, guillotines from the French Revolution, and the mecca it had eventually become for painters and artists. He would stop and deliver each piece of history as if it were as dear to him as his own dog.

As we walked, I noticed a girl on our tour who seemed about fourteen, the same age I'd been on my first trip abroad. She was with her father, dragging her feet slowly as we made our way up the hill toward the Sacré-Coeur. I overheard her complaining about being tired and wanting to go back to the hotel.

Feeling bold, I asked her, "First time to Europe?"

She weakly replied, "Yeah."

I looked straight into her eyes. "You can sleep when you're dead."

The girl's own eyes widened.

I continued to tell her she might not get this opportunity again. To travel. To see the world. Especially with her dad. I also told her a story I'm sure she didn't care to hear, about how I, too, as a teenager, had dragged my feet on my first trip abroad. But now I was ready to grasp each moment. How I'd brought my boyfriend to London when I was just seventeen when my parents were teaching a study abroad program. How traveling had changed his perspective too. How he then had become determined to make travel a lifelong priority. How that boyfriend was now my husband. How we now live abroad and—yeah, sleep is important, but so is taking the opportunity to see the world when you have the chance. I don't know if what I said resonated with her, but I had a feeling that one day, like it had with me, it might.

Behind her, the girl's father mouthed a thank-you to me.

The tour ended at the top of the hill of Montmartre with a sweeping view of Paris, the sun just about to make its way past the horizon. I was tired. But, taking my own advice, I headed to the Eiffel Tower. A hook was inside me, pulling me to keep going. Plus, I needed to thank the Iron Lady.

I found a spot on the grass among hundreds of others to watch the show. I didn't feel embarrassed or scared to be alone. I didn't feel alone at all, really. As soon as the Eiffel Tower started glittering against the inky black sky, I whispered to myself, "We did it. We moved abroad. And here I am, writing about my travels for a living. It's weird, but it's wonderful."

All those years ago, the man at the Amsterdam windmill bar had told me that working fifty hours a week was criminal. Not long after, Michael and I had watched the Eiffel Tower light up before us and I'd vowed to make a change. We don't always follow through on every dream or wish we make. But for me, being here now was the proof that I had, that Michael and I had. We were two people who had veered off the conventional path and chosen adventure—albeit well-researched, strategically planned adventure.

Moving abroad didn't just serve as a catalyst for my self-discovery; it also helped me unearth what I wanted out of life. As a native Texan, I never thought I'd live anywhere else, and I'd only ever dreamed of what I thought was written in the stars: marriage, home, children, a career.

I knew now that leaving doesn't mean you have to give those things up. But staying behind can sometimes mean giving up on dreams you didn't even know you had. It's not that I think everyone has to move across the world to figure out what they want out of life. Traveling doesn't have to mean abandoning everything you know and starting somewhere new. Even small adventures outside your comfort zone can change your perspective. Because maybe you're destined to stay in your hometown and start a stone-fruit farm. Maybe you'll make the best peach cobbler on earth—and if that's the case, I'll take two pies, please.

But I understand now that I can dream bigger. I didn't have to stick with the same lifestyle that everyone around me seemed content to slip into when it didn't feel right for me, even when self-doubt crept in and I wasn't always sure of myself or my chosen path. I realized that I could have the best of both worlds—I could live an unconventional life while still enjoying conventional comforts. I still had my mortgage and my picket fence. But I didn't feel held back by them.

We all grow up based on the influences around us. Sometimes we can't help who we are or the circumstances we're in. But small choices can spark the beginning of change. Through all the mishaps and all the luck, all the bureaucracies and adventures, I've learned so far that a life well lived comes down to figuring out exactly what you want.

Then doing absolutely everything you can to get it.

Helene, Michael, Hugo, and Millie on their way to Germany

*Spain, Paris, and Prague with Helene's parents,
Nina and Craig Flournoy*

Christmas market in Basel, Switzerland

Almabtrieb festival in Austria

Inspiration

They say a picture is worth a thousand words, but maybe they haven't read these books. Here are some of my favorite books and movies that have inspired me to travel and live out my dreams.

BOOKS

- *The Alchemist* by Paulo Coelho
- *The Innocents Abroad* by Mark Twain
- *The 4-Hour Workweek: Escape 9-5, Live Anywhere, and Join the New Rich* by Tim Ferriss
- *A Year in Provence* by Peter Mayle
- *Outliers: The Story of Success* by Malcolm Gladwell
- *A Moveable Feast* by Ernest Hemingway
- *What I Was Doing While You Were Breeding: A Memoir* by Kristin Newman
- *Travels with Charley: In Search of America* by John Steinbeck
- *Germany: Memories of a Nation* by Neil MacGregor
- *Wild: From Lost to Found on the Pacific Crest Trail* by Cheryl Strayed
- *Travel as a Political Act: A Radical Guide to Meaningful Travel* by Rick Steves

MOVIES

- *Midnight in Paris*
- *Pride and Prejudice*
- *Before Sunrise*
- *Miracle on 34th Street*
- *The Sound of Music*
- *Under the Tuscan Sun*
- *Roman Holiday*
- *Mamma Mia!*
- *The Secret Life of Walter Mitty*
- *My Fair Lady*
- *An American in Paris*
- *Magic in the Moonlight*
- *Love Actually*
- *Life is Beautiful*

Acknowledgments

My editor, Avalon Radys, told me not to try to thank everyone by name because I would forget someone. So, I won't. But a few people made this book possible and have to be mentioned.

Thank you to Todd Wildman for remembering me from high school and recommending me as an author. Thank you, Blue Star Press, for thinking my story was good enough to share and making my dreams come true. Thank you to my incredible (and patient) editors, Lindsay Wilkes-Edrington and Avalon Radys, for pushing me and believing in me. Without your invaluable feedback, guidance, and expertise, this book would have not been possible. Your keen eyes and knack for finding the right stories are unmatched.

To my friends and family, you know who you are. Thank you for being part of my story. Specifically, the world's best girlfriends—the 229 girls: Lori, Jordan, Michelle, Christina, Biss, and Colleen. And Kelly, Sarah, Maddie, Sara, Taylor (and Josh!), who are sprinkled throughout this book. Thank you for always being there for me. My sisters, Louise and Emma. My German friends, Robert, Andrea,

Abdul, Letizia, and countless others who made Heidelberg feel like home.

Thank you to my dogs, Hugo and Millie, who listened to me (and licked my face) as I laughed and cried when I felt like all was lost. Moving y'all abroad was the most difficult and rewarding process.

A sincere thanks to my online community and blog readers for being part of my journey, for your support, kind words, and encouragement. I am super pumped and honored you bought this book (even you, Angela). I appreciate y'all so much. Michael is drinking a glass of milk in your honor.

Thank you to the continent of Europe. I really can't believe you're a real place, and my life will be a lifelong love letter to you.

To Michael's mom and dad, Jim and Jan Sula—thank you for raising Michael and believing in us and our wild dreams. Jan, I know you'd be proud, and I think of you whenever I enter a church. Which is more than you'd probably think. There are a lot of beautiful ones in Europe.

Again, thank you to my parents, Nina and Craig Flournoy, who spent the better part of a year helping me write this book and being behind-the-scenes editors even though you weren't paid. I owe you my life. Literally. You are my heroes and the smartest people I know. I can't believe I am lucky enough to call y'all my parents. Like it or not, you gave me the confidence to believe I could do anything I set my mind to, which sometimes means changing continents.

Mom, thank you for emboldening me to go out and discover the world, for giving me the nudge to keep going to one more city, one more Christmas market, one more café. Despite writing your own books and articles, you took time out of your life to help me with mine. Whenever I see the moon, I see you.

Dad, you were right: writing isn't fun; it's the having written part that is. Thanks for buying me *The Iliad* and *The Odyssey* when I was seven. I think you knew I would always be up for an adventure. You are a Mad Dog, but dogs are the best, after all.

Lastly, Michael, I owe you the world. Thank you for listening to me read each chapter to you aloud while you drove across the country. Thank you for giving me the space and time and encouragement to write this book. Your zest for life is contagious. You are the world's greatest human, and for some reason, you chose to spend life with me.

Michael and Helene in Strasbourg
Notice the patched-up hole in his coat?

Helene Sula is an American travel writer and blogger. Though she grew up fearful of change, travel inspired Helene to get outside her comfort zone. Now she aims to motivate others to have their own eye-opening adventures, pursue their passions, and expand their boundaries, even if they're still figuring out what those are.

She has traveled to more than fifty countries (and counting), blogging about her one-of-a-kind travel adventures focused on historical and cultural experiences, local cuisines, and off-the-beaten-path destinations along the way. Her writing has been featured in *Business Insider*, *Forbes*, *People*, and more.

Originally from Texas, Helene now resides in Oxford, United Kingdom with her husband, Michael, and their two adventure-loving pups, Hugo and Millie. When she's not trotting the globe or posting captivating travel content, you can find her exploring Oxford's hidden gems.